Assessing Landscape Dynamics Using Multitemporal Remotely Sensed Imagery in the Sonoran Desert Network

Natural Resource Technical Report NPS/SODN/NRTR—2011/513

Authors

Miguel L. Villarreal
School of Natural Resources and the Environment
The University of Arizona

Willem van Leeuwen
Raul Romo
Arizona Remote Sensing Center
Office of Arid Lands Studies
Geography and Regional Development
The University of Arizona

J. Andrew Hubbard
Sonoran Desert Network
National Park Service
7660 E. Broadway Blvd., #303
Tucson, AZ 85710

Editing and Design

Alice Wondrak Biel
Sonoran Desert Network
National Park Service
7660 E. Broadway Blvd., #303
Tucson, AZ 85710

September 2011

U.S. Department of the Interior
National Park Service
Natural Resource Stewardship and Science
Fort Collins, Colorado

The National Park Service's Natural Resource Stewardship and Science office, in Fort Collins, Colorado, publishes a range of reports that address natural resource topics of interest and applicability to a broad audience in the National Park Service and others in natural resource management, including scientists, conservation and environmental constituencies, and the public.

The Natural Resource Technical Report Series is used to disseminate results of scientific studies in the physical, biological, and social sciences for both the advancement of science and the achievement of the National Park Service mission. The series provides contributors with a forum for displaying comprehensive data that are often deleted from journals because of page limitations.

All manuscripts in the series receive the appropriate level of peer review to ensure that the information is scientifically credible, technically accurate, appropriately written for the intended audience, and designed and published in a professional manner. Data in this report were collected and analyzed using methods based on established, peer-reviewed protocols and were analyzed and interpreted within the guidelines of the protocols.

Views, statements, findings, conclusions, recommendations, and data in this report do not necessarily reflect views and policies of the National Park Service, U.S. Department of the Interior. Mention of trade names or commercial products does not constitute endorsement or recommendation for use by the U.S. Government.

This report is available from the Sonoran Desert Network website, http://www.nature.nps.gov/im/units/sodn/, and at the Natural Resource Publications Management web site, http://www.nature.nps.gov/publications/nrpm/.

Please cite this publication as:

NPS 960/110599, September 2011

Contents

Figures

Tables

Acronyms

CART	classification and regression tree
COST	cosine of theta model
DEM	digital elevation model
DN	digital number
DOQQ	digital ortho quarter quads
ESRI	Environmental Systems Research Institute
EVI	Enhanced Vegetation Index
EVI2	Enhanced Vegetation Index 2
GCP	ground control point
GIS	geographic information systems
GS	Gramm-Schmidt
m	meter
MKT	Multi-temporal Kauth-Thomas
MLC	maximum likelihood classification
MRLC	Multi-resolution Land Characteristics Consortium
MSAVI	Modified Soil Adjusted Vegetation Index
MSS	multispectral scanner system
NDSVI	Normalized Difference Senescent Vegetation Index
NDVI	Normalized Difference Vegetation Index
NDWI	Normalized Difference Wetness Index
NED	National Elevation Dataset
NHP	national historical park
NIR	near infrared
NLCD	National Land Cover Dataset
NPS	National Park Service
NVC	National Vegetation Classification
PC	principal component
SATVI	Soil Adjusted Total Vegetation Index
SAVI	Soil-Adjusted Vegetation Index
SODN	Sonoran Desert Network
SSURGO	Soil Survey Geographic Dataset
TM	thematic mapper
USGS	U.S. Geological Survey
WDVI	Weighted Difference Vegetation Index

1 Introduction

1.1 Background

The Sonoran Desert Network (SODN) is one of 32 National Park Service (NPS) inventory and monitoring (I&M) networks nationwide that are implementing vital signs monitoring in order to assess the condition of park ecosystems and develop a stronger scientific basis for stewardship and management of natural resources across the National Park System. Vital signs, as defined by the I&M Program, are selected physical, chemical, and biological elements and processes of park ecosystems that represent the overall health or condition of a park. Vital-signs monitoring can lead to early detection of potential problems, allowing park managers to take steps to restore ecological health of park resources before serious damage can happen. Landscape Dynamics is one of the vital signs the network has identified for monitoring at 11 park units throughout Arizona and New Mexico. Within the scope of this vital sign, park managers identified landscape fragmentation and land use/land cover patterns around parks as important resource concerns.

Effective protocols for landscape-dynamics monitoring generally use remote sensing and Geographic Information Systems (GIS) to model broad-scale patterns and temporal changes occurring in and around national parks. Protocol development for long-term monitoring of landscape dynamics of SODN parks involves identification of (1) appropriate remote-sensing data for monitoring, (2) image classification and processing schemes, and (3) statistical and spatial analysis techniques to describe change and pattern. The landscape dynamics monitoring protocol presented in this document includes phases of data acquisition, processing, classification, and accuracy assessment. The protocol is based on literature review and expert knowledge.

The aim of this pilot study and protocol development was to retrospectively map land cover and vegetation and characterize historical landscape dynamics of selected areas in and around Tumacácori National Historical Park (NHP), the upper Santa Cruz River, and the surrounding watershed using (1) historical aerial photography and image interpretation and (2) statistical analysis and classification of satellite imagery. The first part of this report includes a literature review of data-acquisition issues, data-preprocessing and quality-assurance steps, attribute and feature generation and extraction, land-cover classification testing, and accuracy assessment and evaluation of maps. The second part describes the methods used to develop a functional landscape dynamics monitoring protocol.

We examined two complementary approaches for monitoring landscape dynamics at multiple spatial and temporal scales: (1) decadal (1987, 1996, and 2006), landscape-scale (1,195 km2), Landsat-derived, land-cover maps; and (2) multi-date (seven years between 1936 and 2006), historical formation maps derived from high-resolution aerial imagery. Although scale, extent, and classification methods for the two approaches differed, the class types were identical and can be analyzed in tandem or separately, depending on park monitoring questions. Our land-cover classification scheme was based on vegetation life forms (tree, shrub, herbaceous) and coarse land-use categories (agriculture and developed). These "formation" classes can be cross-walked to reflect more traditional land-cover classes, for instance, Anderson Classification Levels (Anderson et al. 1976), and have the additional benefit of sharing class attributes with park maps currently being created by the U.S. Geological Survey–NPS Vegetation Characterization Program (http://biology.usgs.gov/npsveg/index.html).

The final section of the report highlights analysis approaches for identifying and monitoring landscape change and fragmentation, and we offer some cursory evaluation of our land-cover data to illustrate the potential use of these data for NPS landscape-dynamics monitoring.

1.2 Literature review

1.2.1 Land-cover classification methods

Many recent satellite imagery classification techniques, data-preprocessing methods, data-product and variable generation, and multi-platform approaches have been reviewed and described in detail in the literature (Collins and Woodcock 1996; Thenkabail et al. 2004; Lu and Weng 2007). In the following section, we highlight some specific approaches and applications relevant to methods developed for the NPS Landscape Dynamics protocol:

- Riparian area and aerial photo accuracy (Yang 2007)

- Image normalization of Landsat Thematic Mapper (TM) (Yang and Lo 2000; Yang and Lo 2002)

- Kauth Thomas Tasseled Cap transforms reflectance data into biophysical parameters like brightness, greenness and wetness or yellowness (Cohen and Goward 2004)

- Multi-temporal Kauth Thomas using two Landsat images to derive seasonal biophysical variables (Collins and Woodcock 1996; Rogan and Yool 2001)

- Sites located in the Montana plains were classified by their departure from mean values in tasseled cap brightness, greenness, and wetness components, and stratified by ecological site description (Maynard et al. 2007)

- Spectral mixture model results (non-photosynthetic vegetation, soil, vegetation) (Roberts et al. 2002); Mixture and decision tree (Roberts et al. 2002)

- Digital elevation model (DEM) + cluster analysis based on spectral data (Munoz-Villers and Lopez-Blanco 2008)

- Classification algorithm comparison (Pal and Mather 2003)

- Supervised classification, post classification in Egypt (Shalaby and Tateishi 2007)

- Mapping detailed biotic communities in the upper San Pedro Valley of Southeastern Arizona using Landsat 7 data and supervised spectral angle classifier (Sohn and Qi 2005)

- Historical data classification (Steyaert and Knox 2008)

- Regional land cover characterization and classification using Landsat TM data and ancillary data sources (Vogelmann et al. 1998)

- Change detection classification and analysis techniques (Coppin et al. 2004; Lu et al. 2004; Zhou et al. 2008)

- Classification and Regression Tree (CART) models have been applied successfully at state and regional levels (C5 decision tree; de Colstoun et al. 2003) and GAP (Gap Analysis Project) Arizona (Lowry et al. 2007). Global decision tree land-cover classification (Friedl et al. 1999; Pal and Mather 2003)

1.2.2 *Feature selection and extraction*

Appropriate feature extraction and selection from remotely sensed data and other environmental variables are critical for optimal land-cover classification (Bruzzone and Serpico 2000; Kuo and Landgrebe 2004). Spatial patterns can be identified based on texture analysis (Haralick et al. 1973; Peddle and Franklin 1991; Dikshit 1996; Bruzzone and Serpico 2000; Franklin et al. 2001). Landscape stratification, combined with topographical and elevation information, has been used successfully in land-cover classifications (Hutchinson 1982; Florinsky 1998), as have spectral indices and transforms, such as Normalized Difference Vegetation Index (NDVI), Enhanced Vegetation Index (EVI), Soil-Adjusted Vegetation Index (SAVI), tasseled cap, and normalized burn ratio (Huang et al. 2002; Cohen and Goward 2004). Multi-temporal Landsat data have been used effectively to incorporate temporal dynamics (e.g., seasonal, interannual) (Coppin and Bauer 1994; Wilson and Sader 2002). Grinand (2008) used a large variety of data and derived geographical layers in combination with CART models for land-cover classification (Grinand et al. 2008) that included soil data, environmental data related to soil formation (McBratney et al. 2003), elevation (m), local slope angle (%), profile curvature, relative hydrological distance to the nearest river (m), relative height to the nearest river (m), spectral reflectance (Landsat), and derived spectral indices and geological data. Based on the recent literature, the CART model generally seems to provide flexible and accurate land-cover classification results and products that can combine remotely sensed spectral data and ancillary geospatial data. We used See5 (C5.0 2.05) to test and develop the use of CART for land-cover classification.

2 Methods

2.1 Vegetation mapping from historical aerial photography

2.1.1 Aerial photography

2.1.1.1 Acquisition and image processing

We collected historical aerial-photography datasets of the study area from various sources with varying levels of pre-processing. Several datasets were procured from the Arizona Geological Survey as hardcopy aerials and scanned to digital format. Other photographs were acquired in digital format from the Arizona Remote Sensing Center, the Santa Cruz County Department of Planning, and the Stromberg Lab at Arizona State University. Acquisition of panchromatic and color-infrared aerial photographs included the following historical aerial photography dates: 1936, 1956, 1959, 1967, 1975, 1984, 1992, 1996, 2004, and 2006. Most aerial photographs had no spatial reference and were georeferenced to digital ortho quarter quads (DOQQs) as references. Georeferencing was conducted using the ESRI ArcMap 9.2 software georeferencing tool, in which a series of common points were selected from the DOQQ images and the historical image to be georeferenced.

2.1.2 Mapping procedures

We acquired baseline vegetation maps of Tumacácori NHP and the Upper Santa Cruz River (Drake et al. 2009) and the Santa Cruz River Riparian Vegetation Map (ARSC&SI 2008). Both maps were created using methods developed for the USGS/NPS Vegetation Characterization Program. During the early mapping stages, the categorical mapping unit for these vegetation maps was the formation level (dominant lifeform), later refined through extensive field work to the alliance level (dominant species) as required by National Vegetation Classification standards (Grossman et al. 1998; FGDC 2008). For land cover-scale mapping and analysis, we classified vegetation to the formation level, which can be easily cross-walked to the Anderson classification scheme commonly used for mapping land use and land cover using multispectral satellite imagery (Anderson et al. 1976).

The methods used to create the NPS and Santa Cruz County maps began with coarse formation maps of relatively homogenous areas identified from high-resolution imagery (Quickbird = 0.6 m). We field-checked the accuracy of the Santa Cruz County formation map (an ~51 km stretch of the Santa Cruz River from Mexico to Pima County) and found it to be highly accurate (kappa = .941, overall accuracy = 95%).[*] With this high accuracy, we felt confident in applying an identical formation mapping technique to historical aerial photographs. We mapped the following 11 formation types: Barren, Agriculture, Herbaceous, Shrub Savanna, Tree Savanna, Shrubland, Wooded Shrubland, Mesquite Woodland, Riparian Woodland, Mesquite Forest, and Riparian Forest.

Watersheds and catchments, defined by topography and hydrology, are logical units for examination of ecological change in river systems (Aspinall and Pearson 2000; Committee on Watershed Management 1999). To standardize and simplify the mapping effort, and because historical-photograph datasets often have incomplete coverage, we mapped formations for 11 vegetation transects within the study area, with each transect stratified geographically by watershed catchment (Figure 2-1). Catchments and associated stream networks were derived from a 10-m NED (National Elevation Dataset) DEM using the ArcGIS ArcHydro extension. One transect was established at the center of each major catchment from the U.S./Mexico border to the Santa Cruz/Pima County border. Each transect was 2.0 × 2.5 km, with the exception of Tumacácori NHP, where we mapped the entire park, including a 100-m buffer. Vegetation and land cover within these transects were mapped for each date of historical aerial photography when available (1936, 1956, 1959, 1967, 1975, 1984, 1992, 1996, and 2004).

2.2 Land-cover classification

2.2.1 Topography

To analyze topography and derive topographic variables for image classification, we used a DEM from the NED archives, administered by the U.S. Geological Survey (USGS). We also obtained digital-raster-graphic, scanned topographic quadrangle maps from the Arizona Remote Sensing Center.

---

[*] Kappa is a measure of agreement between map classification data and reference data. Kappa values range from -1.0 (complete disagreement) to 1.0 (perfect agreement).

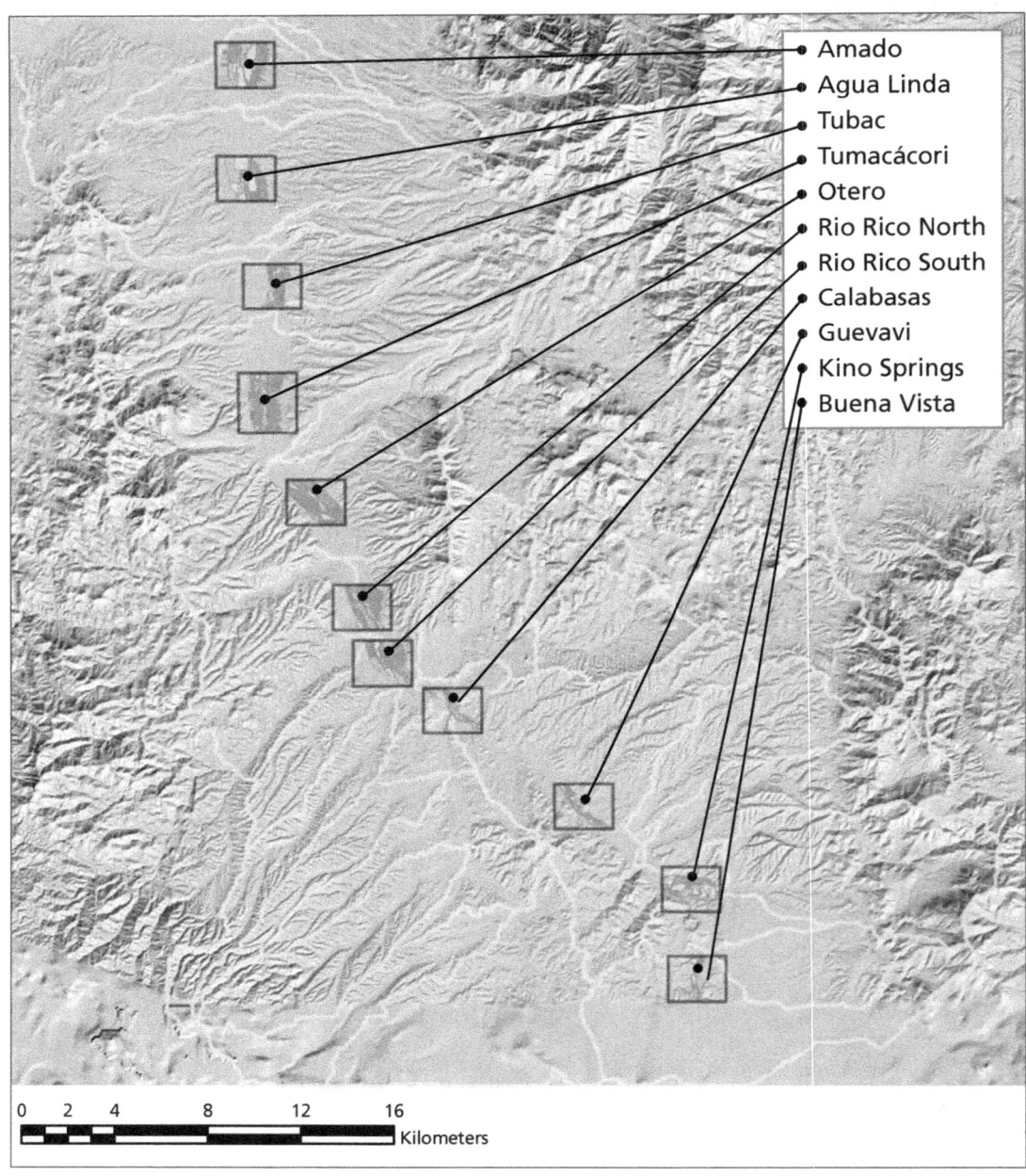

- Amado
- Agua Linda
- Tubac
- Tumacácori
- Otero
- Rio Rico North
- Rio Rico South
- Calabasas
- Guevavi
- Kino Springs
- Buena Vista

0   2   4   8   12   16
Kilometers

Figure 2-1. Location of area transects used for mapping activities. The area transects were located at the center of each major catchment (yellow lines) from the U.S./Mexico border to the Santa Cruz/Pima County border.

2.2.2 Landsat

2.2.2.1 Acquisition

We selected multi-year Landsat scenes (path 36, row 38) as one of the main datasets for monitoring landscape dynamics of Tumacácori NHP. The Landsat TM 5 images used were acquired at approximately 10-year intervals from 1987 to 2006 (May 3 and September 8, 1987; May 11 and August 31, 1996; and May 23 and August 27, 2006). The two Landsat scenes from 2006 were purchased from the USGS; data from 1987 and 1996 were acquired from the Arizona Regional Image Archive. We used pre- and post-growing season scenes to exploit spectral change related to plant phenology changes that occur during the summer months following rains from the southwestern monsoon.

2.2.2.2 Image preprocessing

Terrain-corrected Level 1L Landsat data, acquired from the Land Processes Distributed Active Archive Center (https://lpdaac.usgs.gov/), require additional processing to improve geometric accuracy and remove atmospheric noise. Accurate geometric registration is important when comparing changes in land-cover pixels over time; atmospheric preprocessing steps are critical for ensuring accurate spectral transformations. Brief descriptions of all the steps that were executed and evaluated to preprocess the data are provided in the following sections.

Orthorectification—. Remotely sensed data usually contain both systematic and unsystematic geometric errors. These errors can be divided into two classes: errors that we can correct using data from platform ephemeris and knowledge of internal-sensor distortion, and errors that cannot be corrected with acceptable accuracy without a sufficient number of ground control points (GCPs). A GCP is a point on the surface of Earth where both image and map coordinates can be identified (Jensen 1996). Those geometric distortions that can be corrected through analysis of sensor characteristics and ephemeris include scan skew, mirror scan velocity non-linearities, panchromatic distortion, spacecraft velocity, and perspective geometry (systematic distortions). Non-systematic distortions that can only be corrected with the use of GCPs are attitude (roll, pitch, and yaw) and altitude (Bernstein 1983; Jensen 1996).

The process of orthorectification can be conducted as an image-to-map rectification or as an image-to-image registration; we chose the latter, using a Multi-resolution Land Characteristics Consortium (MRLC) product to orthorectify our Landsat images. The image-to-image registration process involves translation and rotation alignment, in which two images of like geometry and the same geographic area are positioned co-incident to one another so that corresponding elements of the same ground area appear on the same place on the registered images (Chen and Lee 1992; Jensen 1996).

For this process, we used an orthorectified image from the MRLC and a 30-m-resolution DEM from the area of interest as spatial references. We used ERDAS Imagine software and followed the standard protocol used by the Arizona Remote Sensing Center for preprocessing Landast 5 images. We utilized the path 36 and row 38 MRLC from June 15, 2000, re-sampled to 30-m resolution, re-projected to UTM Zone 12, with datum NAD83 and spheroid GRS 1980. For each of the images we orthorectified, we used at least 30 GCPs, obtaining an accuracy of less than a one-half-pixel error (Table 2-1).

Table 2-1. Number of ground control points and root mean square error for each date processed.

Date	GCPs (n)	RMS error
May 3, 1987	32	0.4034
September 8, 1987	30	0.3329
May 11, 1996	32	0.4322
August 31, 1996	30	0.1774
May 23, 2006	31	0.4874
August 37, 2006	32	0.3649

Radiometric and atmospheric correction—. Ideally, the radiant flux recorded by the bands of a remote-sensing system is an accurate representation of the radiant flux leaving the feature of interest (e.g., soil, vegetation, water). However, errors can enter the data-collection system during data acquisition. One example is radiometric error. In remote sensing, radiometric error can be introduced by the sensor system itself if the individual detectors are not properly functioning or calibrated. The intervening atmosphere between our target (feature of interest) and the remote-sensing system may also introduce error. Some atmospheric processes, such as atmospheric attenuation, can obscure the data to the point where the energy recorded by the remote sensor does not resemble the energy that was originally reflected from the target in the terrain (Jensen 1996). Atmospheric effects on wavebands (including scattering and absorption phenomena) are both additive and multiplicative in nature (Curcio 1961; Turner et al. 1971; Sibins 1978; Slater et al. 1983; Chavez 1996).

Algorithms that address radiometric and atmospheric errors of remote-sensing data aim to suppress error introduced by the sensor and noise introduced by atmospheric processes. To complete the atmospheric and radiometric correction in our data, we applied the cosine-of-theta (COST) model proposed by Chavez (1996), using Landsat TM bands 1–5 and 7, to each of the images used in this project. The data requirements to run the model are:

- Minimum digital number (DN) value per band in the Landsat image (DN from the darkest value per Landsat band).

- Sun elevation angle for the time the image was acquired (given in degrees).

- Sun–earth distance for the time the image was acquired (given in astronomical units).

- Chavez's (1996) improved dark-object atmospheric correction for Landsat TM5 multispectral data (bands 1–5 and 7). Below is the general structure of the model for Band 1 of Landsat TM (each band is processed with different coefficients; however, sun–earth distance and sun angle remain the same). Each band is processed according to different coefficients that vary:

    MODEL = $((-L_{haze} + (0.0602353 \times (TM$ Reflectance band1) $- 0.15)) \times PI \times$ Sun-Earth Distance^2) $/ (195.7 \times COS (PI/180 \times (90 -$ Sun-Angle)) ^{2}), where L_{haze} is a coefficient that has to be calculated for each band in each image.

To account for more recent sensor degradation, we utilized new correction factors and coefficients presented by Chander et al. (2007). We used an MS Excel spreadsheet to calculate the inputs for the equation above and input the coefficients into an ERDAS Imagine graphical model to transform the original images into atmospherically corrected images. We applied this methodology to each of the orthorectified images to remove atmospheric and radiometric noises.

Multi-temporal scene normalization—. We tested radiometric scene normalization schemes in an attempt to reduce variance between multitemporal images introduced by residual atmospheric noise and sensor degradation. When normalizing an image, the general approach is to apply a set of model parameters derived from a linear-regression model describing the relationship between reflectance values from stable targets located on reference and non-reference scenes (i.e., bright and dark objects that do not show large variability in reflectance from scene to scene). However, our results showed that this normalization introduced more uncertainty in the data, particularly related to temporal variability introduced by apparent "dark," barren target pixels that may have, in fact, had vegetation present. Therefore, we did not implement normalization in this classification process. We do believe, however, that normalization is an important step when dealing with multi-temporal datasets, and warrants more investigation and potential inclusion in future NPS landscape dynamics monitoring protocols.

2.2.2.3 Image classification

Creation of classification attributes and variables—.Using the orthorectified and atmospheric-radiometric corrected Landsat imagery, we derived the attributes to be used for the land-cover classification (Table 2-2). We generated a number of information layers from the Landsat data acquisitions (6 spectral bands/image; 2 images/year). Many of the following variables were generated using a graphical model in ERDAS Imagine:

- *Landsat reflectance*: Unmodified (but orthorectified and atmospheric-radiometric corrected) six bands from the Landsat 5 sensor. We did not use band 6 (thermal) because the 60-meter resolution is coarser than that of the rest of the bands.

- *Normalized Difference Vegetation Index (NDVI)*: Standard procedure to detect vegetation responses based on Landsat bands 3 and 4, red and near infrared (NIR) reflectance data, respectively.

- *Soil Adjusted Vegetation Index (SAVI)*: A vegetation index similar to NDVI but adjusted by a coefficient (L=0.5) meant to minimize the effects of soil spectral properties (Huete 1988).

Table 2-2. List of Landsat-derived attributes generated from corrected reflectance data.

Variable name	Acronym	Equation*	Reference
Normalized Difference Vegetation Index	NDVI	(NIR-RED)/(NIR+RED)	Tucker 1979
Soil Adjusted Vegetation Index	SAVI	(NIR-RED*(1-L))/(NIR+RED+L)	Huete 1988
Enhanced Vegetation Index	EVI	(G*(NIR-RED))/(NIR+C1*RED-C2*BLUE+L)	Huete et al. 2002
Enhanced Vegetation Index 2	EVI2	2.5* (NIR-RED)/(NIR+2.4RED+1)	Jiang et al. 2007
Modified Soil Adjusted Vegetation Index	MSAVI	((2NIR+1)-((2NIR+1)2-8(NIR-RED))0.5)/2	Qi et al. 1994
Normalized Difference Water Index	NDWI	(NIR-SWIR)/(NIR+SWIR)	Gao 1995
Soil Adjusted Total Vegetation Index	SATVI	((1+L)(Band5-Band3)/(Band5+Band3+L))-(Band7/2)	Marsett et al. 2006
Principal Components	PC		Fung and LeDrew 1987
Tasseled Cap	TC		Crist and Cicone 1984
Texture Analysis	TEXTURE		Haralick et al. 1973; Peddle and Franklin 1991; Dikshit 1996; Bruzzone and Serpico 2000; Franklin et al. 2001
Multi-temporal Kauth-Thomas	MKT		Collins and Woodcock 1996

*These variables were computed using the ERDAS modeler. Principal Components, Tasseled Cap Analysis, Texture analysis, and Multi-temporal Kauth-Thomas (Multi-temporal Tasseled Cap) procedures are addressed in the literature cited above.

- *Soil Adjusted Total Vegetation Index (SATVI):* This index results from the application of a correction factor to the Normalized Difference Senescent Vegetation Index (NDSVI). This index was found to be sensitive to both green and senescent vegetation, which is ideal for rangeland canopy estimates (Marsett et al. 2006).

- *Enhanced Vegetation Index (EVI):* The EVI was developed to optimize the vegetation signal with improved sensitivity in high biomass regions and improved vegetation monitoring through a de-coupling of the canopy background signal and a reduction in atmosphere influences (Huete et al. 2002).

- *Enhanced Vegetation Index 2 (EVI2):* EVI2 is computed without a blue band. It is functionally equivalent to the EVI, although slightly more prone to aerosol noise, which may become less significant with continuing advancements in atmosphere correction (Jiang et al. 2008).

- *Modified Soil Adjusted Vegetation Index (MSAVI):* A modified SAVI (MSAVI) that

replaces the constant L in the SAVI equation with a variable L function. The L function may be derived by induction or by using the product of the NDVI and Weighted Difference Vegetation Index (WDVI): $L = 1 - 2y$ $NDVI \times WDVI$: where y is the soil line parameter (Qi et al. 1994). For this project, we derived the L by induction.

- *Normalized Difference Wetness Index (NDWI):* uses the near-IR (band 4; 0.78–0.90 µm) and a SWIR (band 5; 1.55–1.75 µm) for sensing of vegetation water content (Hardisky et al. 1983; Gao 1995).

- *Tasseled Cap (brightness, greenness, wetness):* Developed by Kauth and Thomas (1976), this index was originally produced to extract information about brightness, greenness, and yellowness of landscapes using the multispectral scanner system (MSS) Landsat sensors. Brightness, the first feature, is a weighted sum of all the bands, and was defined in the direction of principal variation in soil reflectance. It thus measures soil brightness or total reflectance. The second feature, Greenness, is a contrast between the near-infrared bands and the visible bands. A third feature, Yellowness, was originally defined in the spectral direction expected to correspond to plant senescence but was subsequently redefined to serve as a haze diagnostic (Kauth et al. 1979; Crist and Cicone 1984). This index was adapted to be used with Landsat TM by Crist and Cicone (1984).

- *Principal Components (PCs)*: Using this technique, we reduce the dimensionality (number of bands/information) of the dataset by deriving the important components from the original six bands. Using two or three principal components reduces noise and sensor-striping while retaining most of the original data variance (Jensen 1996). The first principal component accounts for the maximum amount of variance of the original dataset. Subsequent principal components account for the remaining variances.

- *Multi-temporal Kauth-Thomas (MKT)*: MKT involves the Gramm-Schmidt (GS) orthogonalization process, which is used to identify the column vectors of a transformation matrix. The method orthogonalizes spectral vectors that are taken directly from a bi-temporal image, in much the same way that the original tasseled-cap transformation was created for single-date imagery. When done carefully, the GS process can produce three stable components corresponding to multi-temporal analogues of Kauth-Thomas Brightness, Greenness, and Wetness dimensions, plus a change component associated with interdate differences (Collins and Woodcock 1996).

- *Variance:* Calculated local pixel variance of Landsat band 3 (red) with a 3 × 3 moving window.

2.2.2.4 Ancillary datasets

In addition to the image-derived variables, we utilized four ancillary, non-image data layers:

Digital Elevation Model: Three layers containing elevation, slope, and aspect from a 30-meter resolution DEM.

Soil Survey Geographic Dataset (SSURGO): Field-mapping methods using national standards were used to construct the soil maps in the SSURGO database.

2.2.3 Classification scheme

We developed a hybrid classification scheme based on the Anderson Classification system and the National Vegetation Classification (NVC) Terrestrial Vegetation Classification Hierarchy (Anderson et al. 1976; Grossman D.H. et al. 1998; FGDC 2008). We used broad NVC physiognomic classes, based on vegetation structure and determined by height and percentages of cover occupied by tree, shrub, and herbaceous strata. We further distinguished class types by modifying the physiognomic system to include additional qualifiers based on elevation and hydrologic attributes (e.g., upland and riparian) (Table 2-3). One benefit of using the physiognomic system is that consecutive stages can be captured within the classification, generating useful information for understanding riparian dynamics. Cultural land cover classes were based on Anderson Level II classes (Table 2-3).

2.2.4 Running the models

2.2.4.1 Training data

One advantage of the NVC physiognomic classification scheme is that it allows the use of high-resolution digital aerial imagery to generate training data and accuracy assessment. The high-resolution satellite imagery and aerial photography (~1-m resolution) commonly used for vegetation mapping allows interpreters to distinguish map classes by estimating lifeform height and percent cover. For this research, we appropriated the NVC classification system, in large part because of the coincident mapping efforts at Tumacácori NHP and the Santa Cruz River described above. The high kappa value associated with these projects (kappa = .941, overall accuracy = 95%) engendered confidence that we could use this information as "training" data for the 2006 CART classification. These known locations are called training sites because their spectral characteristics are used to "train" the image-classification algorithm (Jensen 1996).

Suitable training sites for the multi-temporal dataset were selected by examining historical aerial imagery (1980, 1983, 1992, 1996 and 2006) to determine areas that exhibit lifeform stability over time. For each class, 25–125 training points were generated, depending on the estimated total amount of area occupied by each class. For example, the Water class, uncommon in the study area, was assigned 27 training points, while Shrubland,

Table 2-3. Comparison of the class types with National Vegetation Classification (NVC) terrestrial vegetation classification hierarchy formations.

ID	Class	Description	Related formation	NVC formation description
1	Agriculture	Row crops, orchards, and pasture	Agriculture	Row crops, orchards, and pasture
2	Barren	Rock, bare soil, and strand	Barren	Rock, bare soil, and strand
3	Upland Forest	Tree cover >60%, non-riparian	Forest	Tree cover >60%, non-riparian
4	Herbaceous	Herbaceous-dominated with sparse tree and shrub cover	Herbaceous	Herbaceous-dominated. Tree cover <10%, shrub cover <10%
5	Industrial/ Commercial	Areas of intensive use with much of the land covered by structures and impervious surfaces	Industrial/ Commercial	Areas of intensive use with much of the land covered by structures and impervious surfaces
6	Riparian Mesquite Forest	Tree cover >60%. Mesquite-dominated and typically found adjacent to river channels	Forest	Tree cover >60%.
7	Woodland	Tree cover dominant cover type but <60% total cover	Woodland	Tree cover dominant cover type but <60% total cover
8	Residential	Areas of high- and low-density residential structures	Residential	Areas of high- and low-density residential structures
9	Riparian Forest	Tree cover >60%. Dominated by cottonwood and Goodding's willow	Forest	Tree cover >60%.
10	Riparian Woodland	Tree cover <60%. Dominated by cottonwood and Goodding's willow/ Netleaf hackberry	Woodland	Tree cover <60%.
11	Shrub Savanna	Herbaceous-dominated with some sparse shrub cover	Shrub Savanna	Herbaceous-dominated, shrub cover present but <10%
12	Shrubland	Shrub/Desert scrub-dominated	Shrubland	Shrub cover >50%
13	Tree Savanna	Herbaceous-dominated with sparse tree cover	Tree Savanna	Herbaceous-dominated, tree cover present but <10%
14	Water	Water	Water	Water

the most prevalent land-cover type, was assigned 122 training points.

2.2.4.2 Classification and regression tree analysis

Classification and regression-tree models have proven useful for land-cover classification and, in many cases, outperformed traditional image classifiers, such as the Maximum Likelihood Classification (MLC) (Hansen et al. 1996; Pal and Mather 2003). CART models are popular for remote-sensing classification in part because the classifier is non-linear and makes no assumptions about data distribution, encouraging the use of spectral and ancillary layers regardless of data scale (Lawrence and Wright 2001). In general terms, by using spectral and ancillary data

as predictor variables and a list of *a priori* selected classes as the response, the model creates a dichotomous "tree" by recursively partitioning training data. The classification-tree rules derived from the training data are then applied directly to variable layers, creating a classified image. Additionally, model accuracy can be increased using CART techniques like "boosting" or "bagging" (Quinlan 1996; Lawrence et al. 2004; Prasad et al. 2006).

Using ArcGIS, sets of training samples and associated x,y coordinates were generated and exported as .txt files. Using these data and the NLCD ERDAS Imagine "Sampling Tool," values were extracted from each input variable and saved as See5 .data and .names files. The See5

CART software requires these two files to construct the model.* We found that the following Classifier Construction options from See5 produced the best models: Boosting (10 trials) and Global Pruning (25%). The See5 CART model is output as a .tree file, which we used to create a land-cover map using the NLCD ERDAS Imagine "See5 Classifier Tool."

2.2.4.3 Evaluation of the CART model using Supervised Classifications

We evaluated the results of the CART model by conducting coincident supervised classifications and comparing the results of the two models. Like the CART process, in a supervised classification the locations of land-cover types are known a priori and samples collected through a combination of field work, analysis of aerial photography, and expert knowledge. The goal is to locate sites representing homogeneous examples of known land-cover types and use the data to train the classifier. We conducted the supervised classification using the same information layers and the same training samples utilized during the CART process.

For comparison purposes, we chose to implement the MLC, one of the most common algorithms used to create supervised classifications. MLC uses the training data to derive a series of multivariate statistics (e.g., means, standard deviations, covariance matrices) and assigns a class to every pixel within and outside the training site based on the statistical likelihood of class membership (Jensen 1996). More specifically, the MLC rule assigns each pixel having pattern measurements or features X to the class c whose units are most probable or likely to have given rise to feature vector X (Swain and Davis 1978; Foody et al. 1992; Jensen 1996). Unlike the CART model, this approach assumes normality (Gaussian distribution) on training-data statistics for each class in each band (Blaisdell 1993; Jensen 1996).

To accomplish the process described above, we used ERDAS to create areas of interest of training data based on training points used for the CART model. We then used the Signature Editor in ERDAS to create the signature file for the supervised classification and merged the derived signature values to create an average class signature per type (e.g., agriculture, forest, industrial), computing a global signature per class derived from the intersection of the signature in our raster input layers.

We executed three MLC supervised classification tests based on the attributes identified in Table 2-4. MLC were performed using the 2006 data only, with each consecutive classification computed using a subset of the original 68 variables. This process was meant to evaluate whether the classification could be refined using key variables as identified from the output CART decision trees. For MLC Test 1, we used all variables used for the CART model. For MLC Test 2, a limited number of variables were used, based on their contribution to the CART classifications. For Test 3, only three variables were used, based on the decision-tree analysis results and an evaluation of which variables had significantly contributed to the explanation and separation of selected land-cover types.

After we were satisfied with our model results, we ran the classifications through a 3 × 3-pixel majority filter. The primary function of the majority filter is to smooth the data, minimizing the single-pixel "salt and pepper" appearance that results from a per-pixel classification.

2.2.5 Accuracy assessment

We assessed map accuracy by randomly generating a set of points and comparing the classified value at those locations to the reference class type and percent cover interpreted from aerial pho-

---

*In order to use the CART/See5 tool developed for ERDAS 8.7, we had to convert every output from the radiometric correction process to signed 16-bit, instead of floating points. In other words, the outputs of the radiometric-correction processes should be set to signed 16-bit, and the same should be applied for the variables extracted from the products in this process (e.g., NDVI, EVI, NDWI). Another important change we made was to redefine the spheroid from GRS 1980 to WGS 84, and the datum from NAD83 to WGS 84, in order to use the same parameters used by the U.S. Forest Service's See5 ERDAS extension. If the SODN plans to use MRLC data for analysis, we will first have to obtain information about how the product was processed. In on our experience, more than one procedure or product type was identified, depending on the year when it was processed. We will also have to know if there was any manipulation of the original data (MRLC product) and adjust our data pre-processing routines accordingly.

tography. We generated 30 points for each class using a random stratified sampling approach. A measure of accuracy for each map was calculated using the kappa statistic (Congalton et al. 2002).

Accuracy points were generated for each CART map, but to reduce time and effort, the same 2006 ground-truth points generated for the 2006 CART map were applied to the 2006 MLC maps.

Table 2-4. Variables used for testing the CART model.

Image date	Variable	Number of bands		
		Test 1	Test 2	Test 3
20060523	EVI2	1		
	EVI	1		
	MSAVI	1		
	NDVI	1	1	
	NDWI	1		
	Principal Components	6	6	
	SATVI	1		
	SAVI	1		
	TM Reflectance	6	6	
	Tasseled Cap	6		
	Image Variance	1	1	1
20060827	EVI2	1		
	EVI	1		
	MSAVI	1		
	NDVI	1	1	
	NDWI	1		
	Principal Components	6	6	
	SATVI	1		
	SAVI	1		
	TM Reflectance	6	6	
	Tasseled Cap	6		
	Image Variance	1	1	1
Multidate	Multi-temporal Kauth-Thomas	12	12	12
NA	Aspect	1		
NA	Elevation	1	1	1
NA	Slope	1		

3 Results

3.1 Assessing historical vegetation change

Based on maps derived from the historical aerial photography (Figure 3-1; figures start on page 16), we summarized and analyzed landscape and patch change within each transect for the time period 1936–2006, using GIS and FRAGSTATS landscape-analysis software. The following figures describe historical change in class area over the entire landscape (i.e., all 11 catchments) (Figure 3-2) and for Tumacácori National Historical Park (Figures 3-3 and 3-4).

From 1956 to 2006, agricultural land decreased in the watershed and was likely replaced by woodland and mesquite forests in various stages of succession (see Figure 3-2). There was a general upward trend in riparian forest and a slight decline in 2006, following the tree die-off that occurred south of the main park unit (see Figure 3-2). Similar trends were evident at Tumacácori NHP as in the overall watershed, but when mapped to 1936 rather than 1956, a few important differences were apparent. For example, mesquite forest class area, highest during 1936, decreased drastically until a general recovery after 1975 (Figure 3-3). Similar trends were evident in riparian woodland and woodland classes (Figure 3-3). The trend shown in riparian forest was similar in both the aerial data and CART classifications (see below)—specifically, a general increase in class area over time and a reduction in the number of patches as riparian forests became more contiguous (Figures 3-3 and 3-4).

3.2 Land-cover classification

3.2.1 Accuracy of classification and regression tree and maximum likelihood classification models

Using the CART model approach, we generated land-cover maps for 2006 (Figure 3-5), 1996 (Figure 3-6), and 1987 (Figure 3-7).

An example of the input variables used to classify Woodland, Residential, and Forest is provided in Figure 3-8.

We identified major differences in the accuracy of the two classification techniques (CART and supervised; see Figure 3-5) when applied to the land-cover classification of the Upper Santa Cruz River Watershed. For the regression tree analysis (CART), we obtained an overall accuracy of 83.8 and a kappa statistic of 0.83. The supervised classification (the best of the three tests) method was less accurate (44.88%, kappa 0.4035) than the CART methodology.* Due to the higher accuracy of the land-cover map generated using the CART model, we decided to derive metrics (e.g., fragmentation, land conversion, connectivity) based on this output.

All CART maps were over 80% accurate: 1987 (85%), 1996 (82%) and 2006 (83%). Individual class accuracies of CART maps varied from 60 to 100% (Appendix A, Table A2). Certain classes were often incorrectly mapped as other classes with similar physiognomic characteristics. For instance, class 4, herbaceous, was most often incorrectly classified as class 13, tree savanna. Both classes are dominated by grass cover, making them difficult to distinguish. While this type of confusion lowered the overall accuracy and kappa values for each map, the errors have no major consequences for landscape-scale analysis and geographic investigation, because the two classes are functionally and ecologically similar at this scale.

The accuracy of land-cover maps created with the CART model was considerably higher the accuracy of those made with the more traditional, supervised Maximum Likelihood Classification and trained with the same dataset (overall accuracies ranged from 21.8 to 44.8 % and Kappas from 0.19 to 0.40). Furthermore, the range of kappas for the MLC maps illustrates one main difference between the CART and MLC approach: CART models can successfully classify using a large number of variables, while accuracies of the MLC maps decreased as the number of variables increased.

---

*The results for our supervised classification, according to overall accuracy and kappa statistics, are shown in Appendix A (Table A1).

3.2.2 Landscape dynamics monitoring

3.2.2.1 Watershed fragmentation indices, 1987–2006

Using the CART land-cover maps from 1987, 1996, and 2006, we calculated several class metrics using the FRAGSTATS program (McGarigal et al. 2002). Landscape-pattern metrics presented in this report fall into the following five groups: Area/Density/Edge, Shape, Core Area, Isolation/Proximity, and Contagion. Several metrics are available within each major group, and FRAGSTATS reports the mean, area weighted mean, median, range, standard deviation, and coefficient of variation for each metric. The number of metrics reported depends on the run parameters selected prior to executing a FRAGSTATS session, with a full set approaching 100 metrics. For illustrative purposes, we selected a few basic metrics from the full set and focused specifically on the mean of each class metric reported. The class metrics presented below (and other relevant metrics) can be analyzed, interpreted, and presented as desired by park or network analysts.

As an illustration, some general trends in land-cover change from 1987 to 2006 have been identified using the fragmentation metrics. For example, there was a general decline in class area of herbaceous and shrubland classes over the time period (Figure 3-9). This is likely explained by the expansion of woody species into grasslands (herbaceous to shrub savanna and shrubland to woodland), a phenomenon observed throughout the Southwest in recent decades. There was also a relatively small but steady increase of indus-trial and residential classes over the time period, which is consistent with rural and urban development trends throughout the southwestern U.S.

In terms of patch complexity, the mean shape index and mean fractal dimension index increased for riparian forest, industrial, and residential classes, indicating that these types became more complex over time (Figures 3-10 and 3-11). The complexity of riparian forest is likely explained by the introduction of effluent wastewater into the system, increasing riparian forest cover since the 1980s. This is also reflected in the mean contiguity index, which indicates that riparian forest patches became more connected over the time period (Figure 3-12). The change in shape complexity of the urban types indicates that development in the area is spatially fragmented and that growing urban areas are becoming increasingly complex.*

3.2.2.2 Urban change map, 1987–2006

By applying post-classification change-detection techniques to CART-derived land-cover maps, we can describe and display land-cover change in a spatially explicit manner. Post-classification change products are created by applying raster algebra to land-cover maps of different dates. Figure 3-13, for example, describes change in pixel values from non-urban to urban between 1987 and 2006. Using this approach, analysts can visually represent changes for any land-cover class of interest. The resulting rasters can be further interpreted and analyzed using GIS. Table 3-1 displays similar information.

---

*The "Water" class was excluded from some analyses because many single, edge/background pixels were misclassified as water (see Figure 3-9). These misclassifications skewed some class statistics and may be addressed in future analysis.

Table 3-1. Change in residential and industrial/commercial land uses, 1987–2006.

Class (1987)	Residential (2006)		Industrial/Commercial (2008)	
	Pixels	Hectares	Pixels	Hectares
Agriculture	1,184	106.56	83	7.47
Barren	5,088	457.92	487	43.83
Herbaceous	2,805	252.45	466	41.94
Industrial/Commercial	-	-	2,683	241.47
Riparian Mesquite Forest	201	18.09	13	1.17
Woodland	6,551	589.59	340	30.6
Residential	17,074	1,536.66	663	59.67
Riparian Forest	191	17.19	9	0.81
Riparian Woodland	497	44.73	56	50.4
Shrub Savanna	2,484	223.56	366	32.94
Shrubland	26,457	2,381.13	914	82.26
Tree Savanna	673	60.51	157	14.13
Total	63,205	5,688.39	6,237	606.69
Total ha converted		4,151.79		319.86

Column on the left indicates the class type in 1987 that was converted to residential or industrial/commercial classes by 2006.

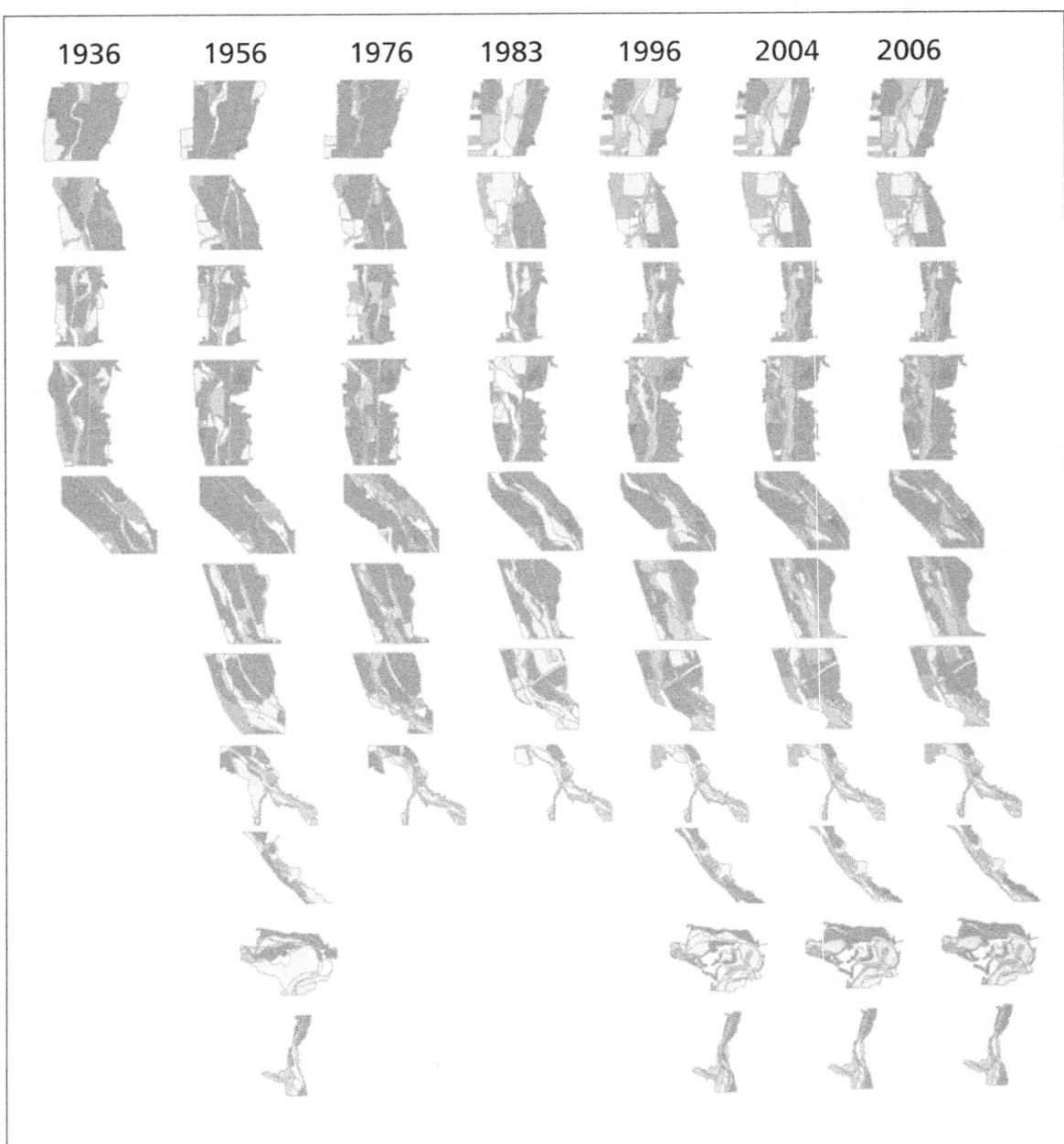

Figure 3-1. Floodplain change, 1936–2006.

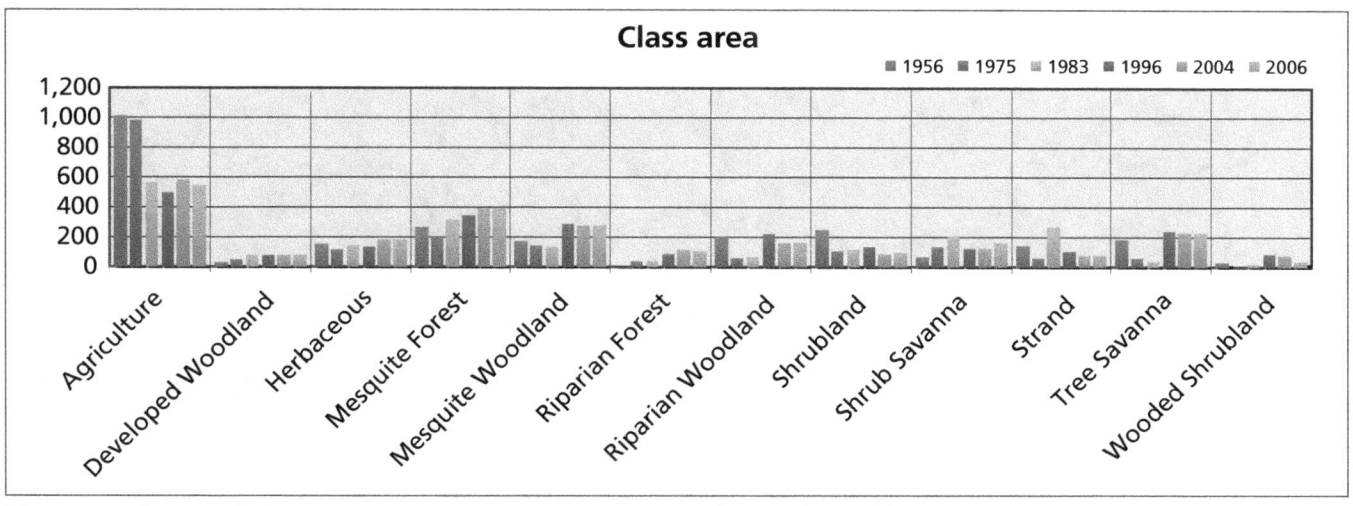

Figure 3-2. Class area in hectares, 1956, 1975, 1983, 1996, 2004 and 2006, derived from aerial photography analysis.

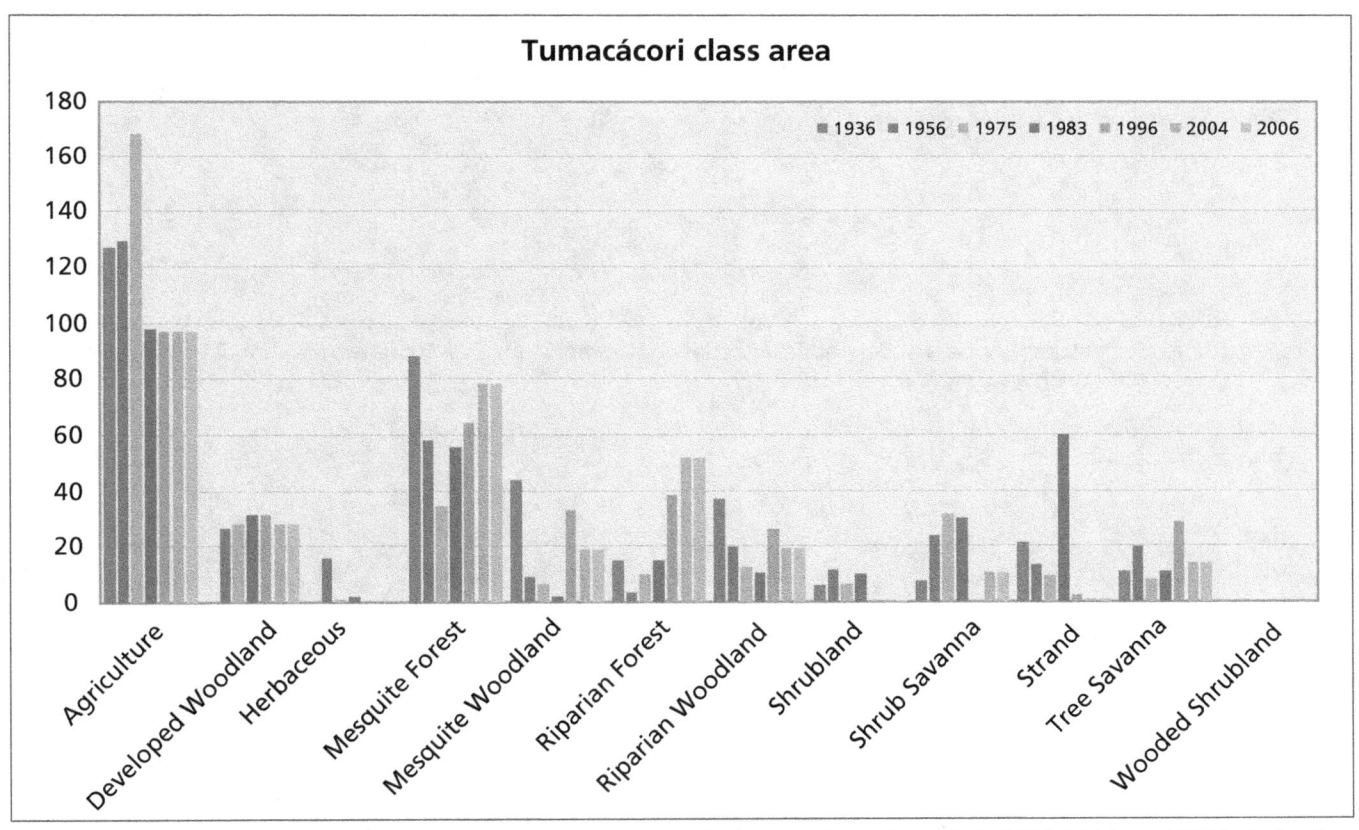

Figure 3-3. Class area distribution for Tumacácori National Historical Park, 1956, 1975, 1983, 1996, 2004, and 2006, derived from aerial photography analysis.

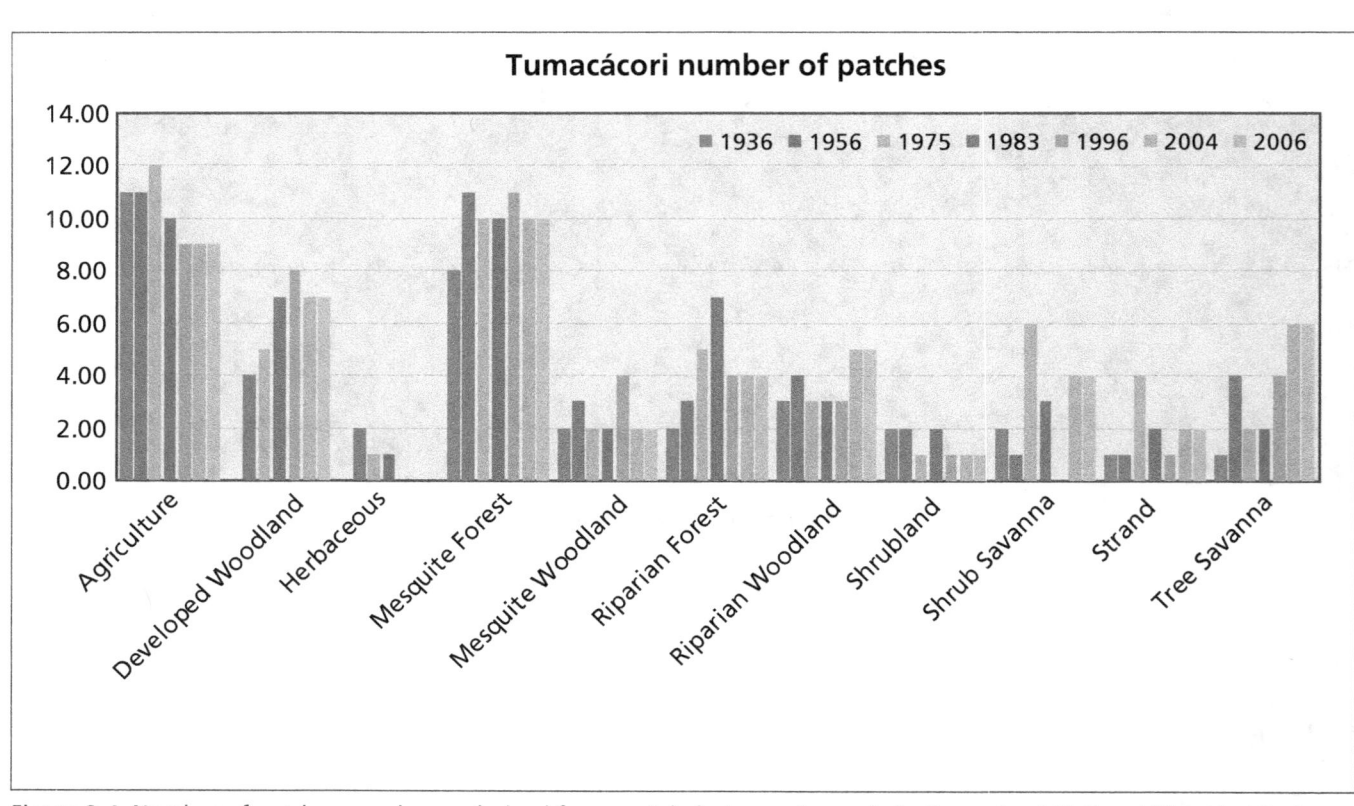

Figure 3-4. Number of patches per class as derived from aerial photography analysis, Tumacácori National Historical Park, 1956, 1975, 1983, 1996, 2004, and 2006.

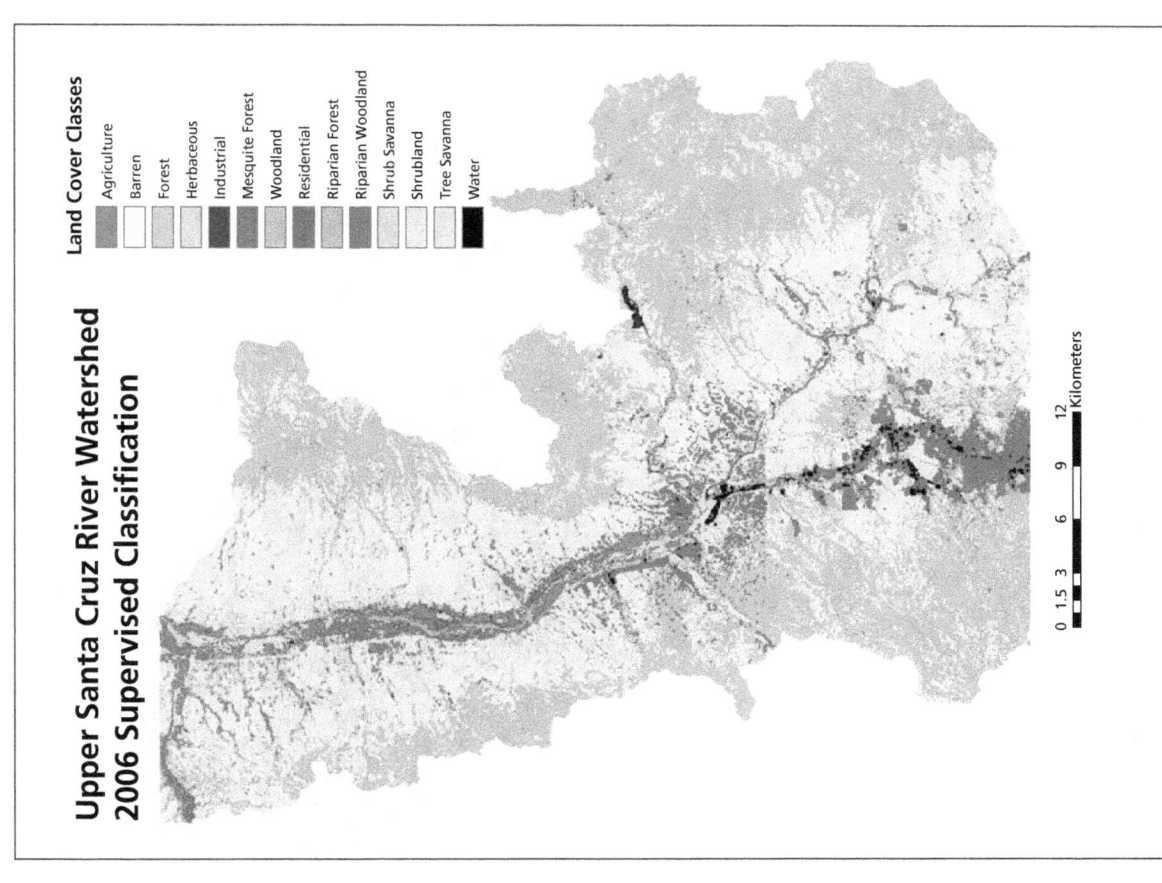

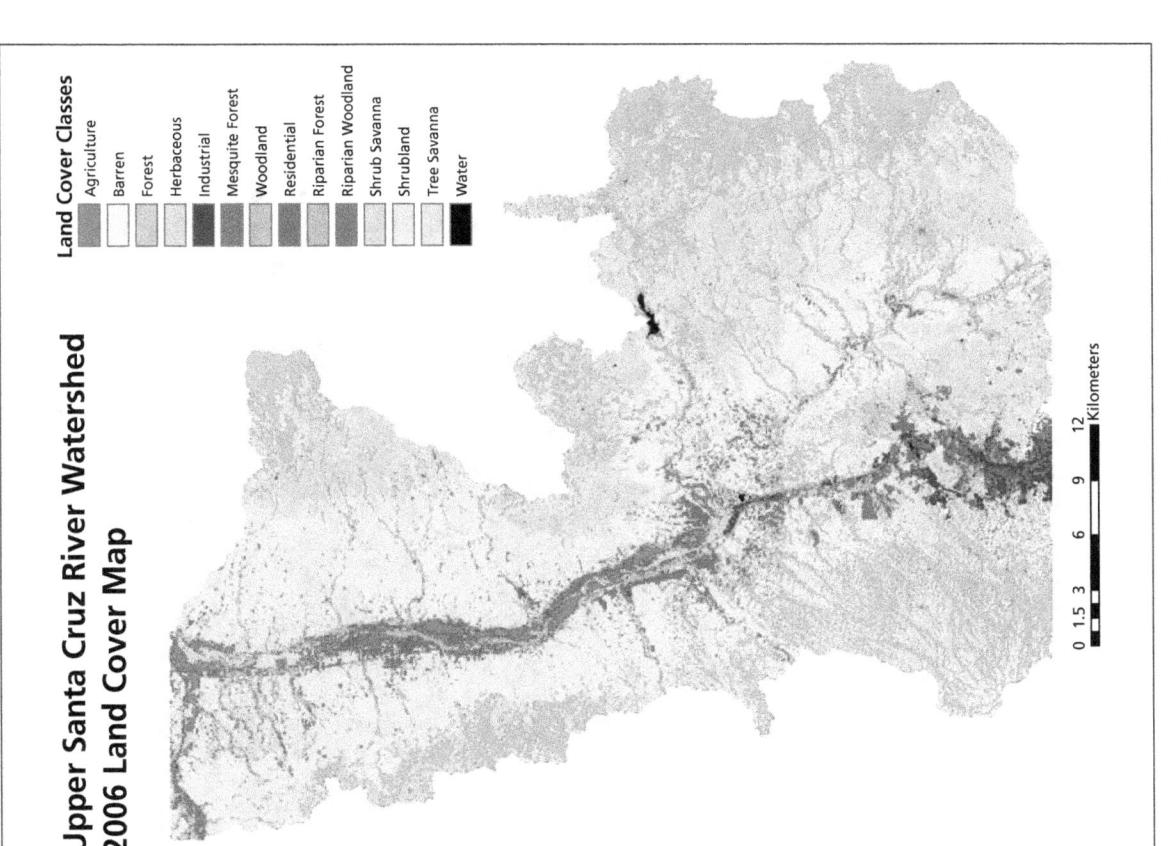

Figure 3-5. Differences between the classification output of CART (left) and the supervised classification (right) for Year 2006.

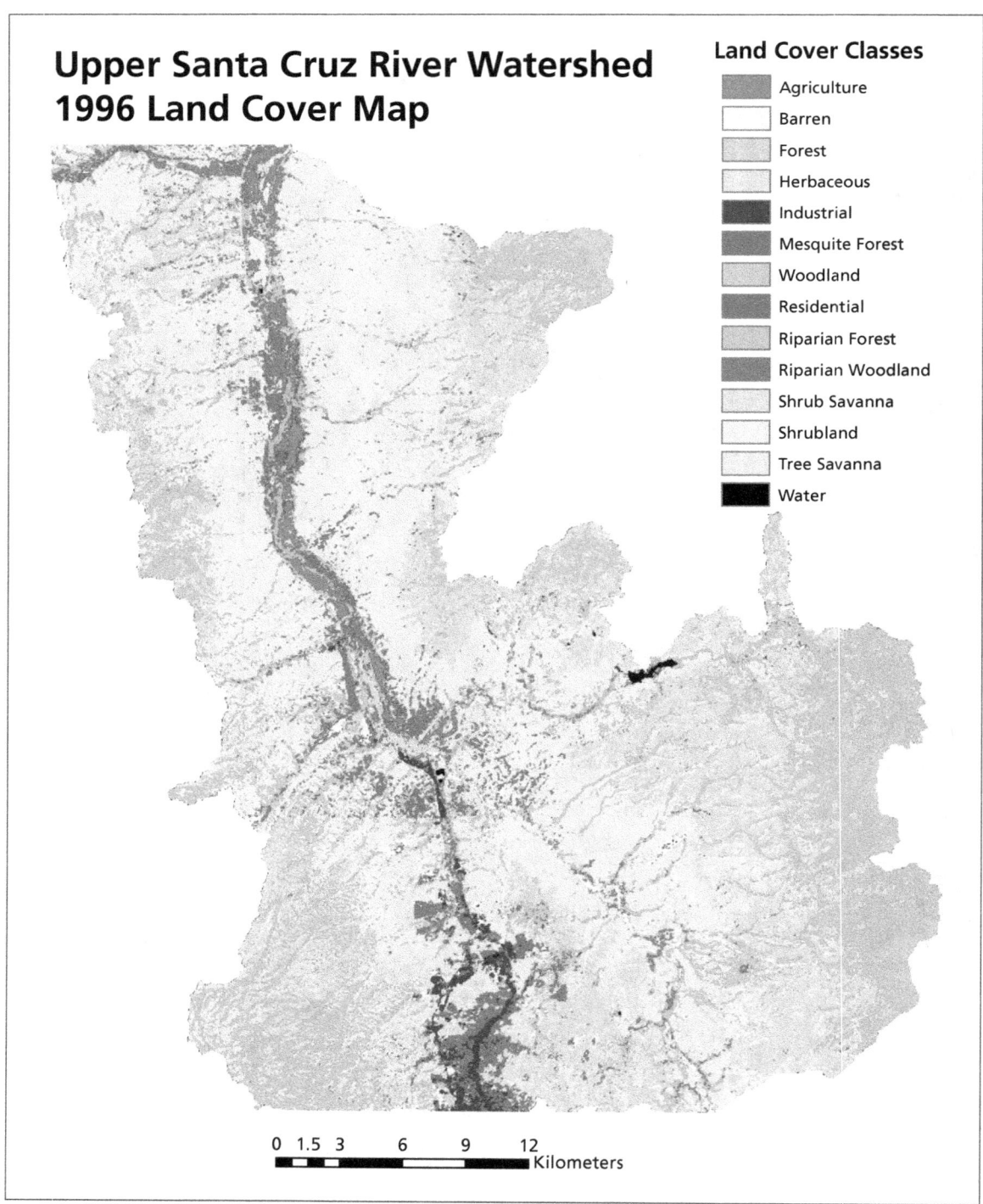

Upper Santa Cruz River Watershed 1996 Land Cover Map

Land Cover Classes

- Agriculture
- Barren
- Forest
- Herbaceous
- Industrial
- Mesquite Forest
- Woodland
- Residential
- Riparian Forest
- Riparian Woodland
- Shrub Savanna
- Shrubland
- Tree Savanna
- Water

0 1.5 3   6   9   12
Kilometers

Figure 3-6. Land-cover map generated using the CART model, 1996.

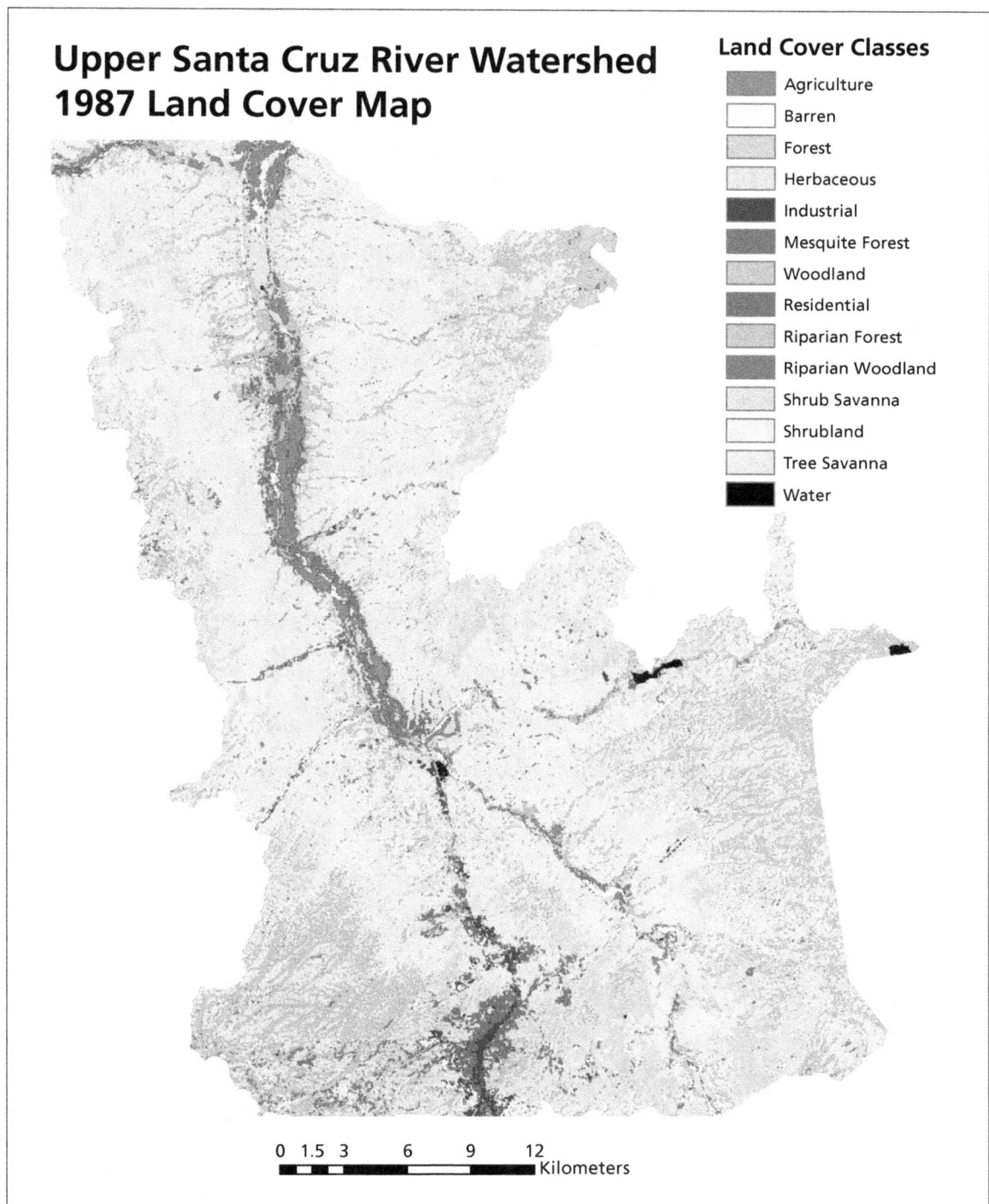

Upper Santa Cruz River Watershed 1987 Land Cover Map

Land Cover Classes

- Agriculture
- Barren
- Forest
- Herbaceous
- Industrial
- Mesquite Forest
- Woodland
- Residential
- Riparian Forest
- Riparian Woodland
- Shrub Savanna
- Shrubland
- Tree Savanna
- Water

0 1.5 3   6   9   12
Kilometers

Figure 3-7. Land-cover map generated using the CART model, 1987.

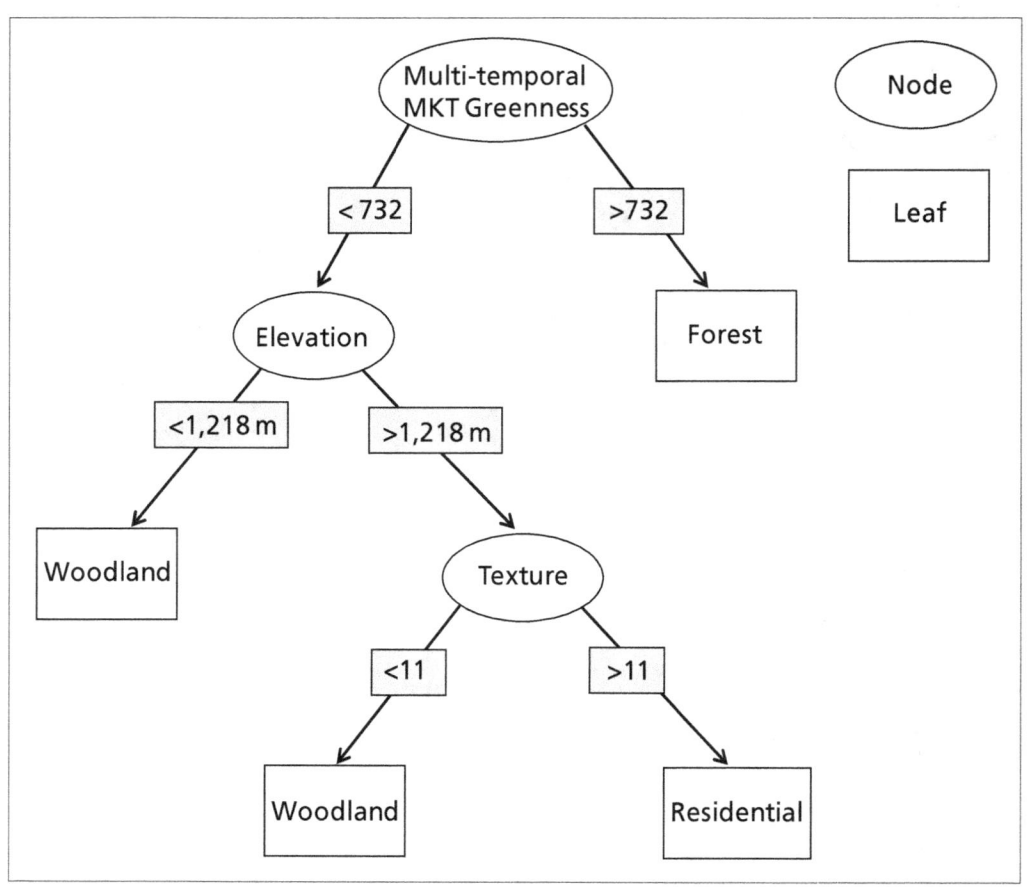

Figure 3-8. Differences between the classification output of CART (left) and the supervised classification (right) for 2006.

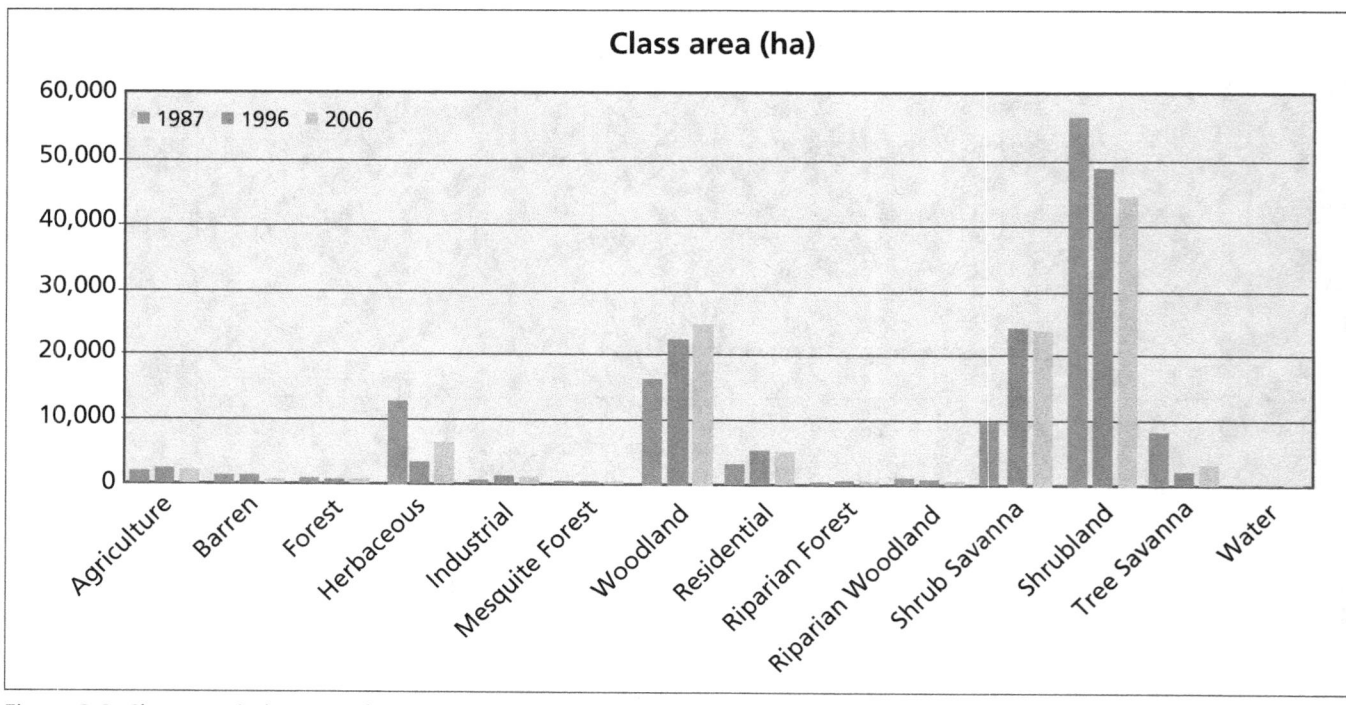

Figure 3-9. Class area in hectares for the 1987, 1996, and 2006 land-cover maps.

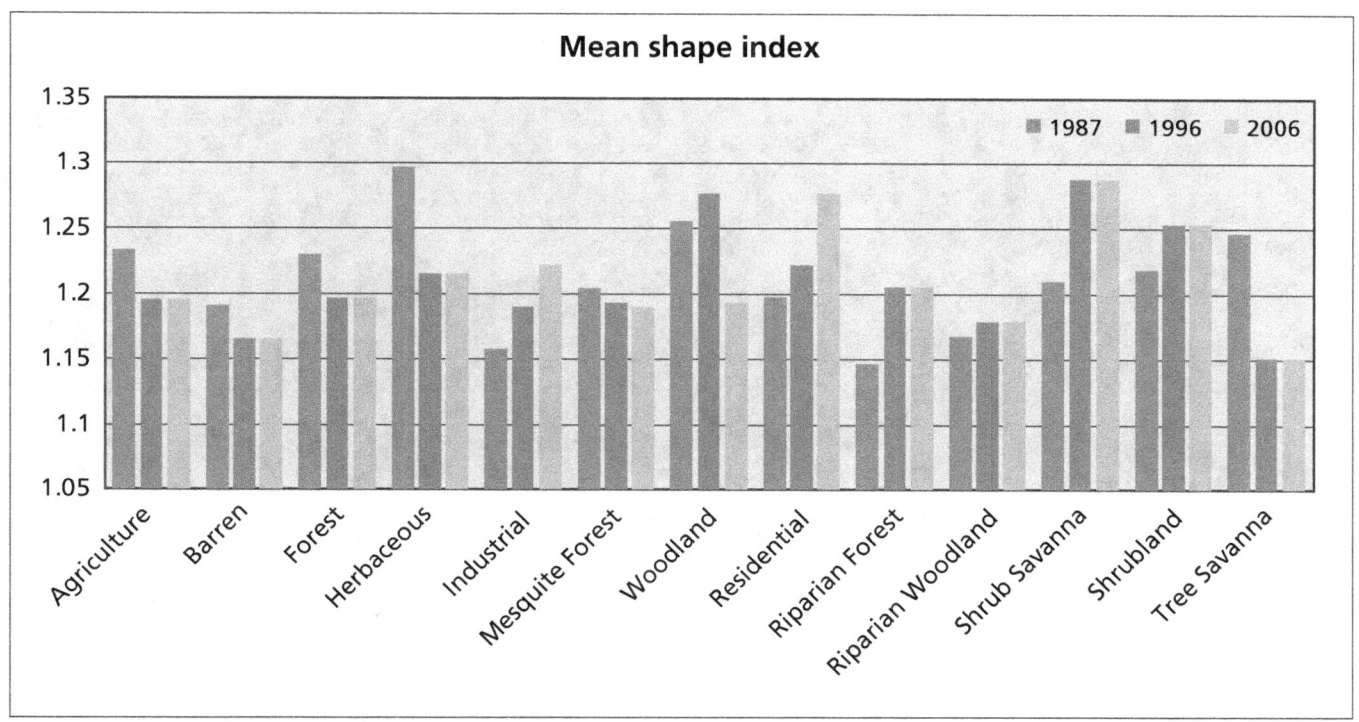

Figure 3-10. Mean shape index for the 1987, 1996, and 2006 land-cover maps.

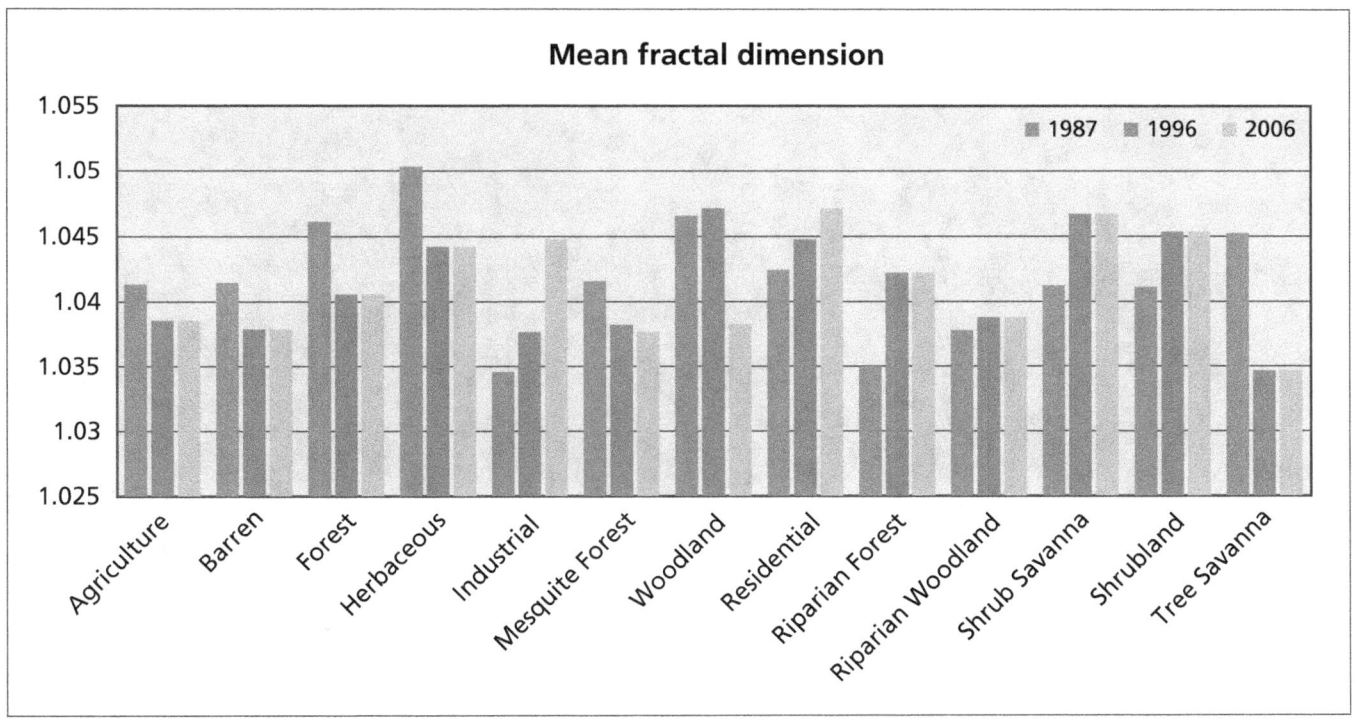

Figure 3-11. Mean fractal dimension index for the 1987, 1996, and 2006 land-cover maps.

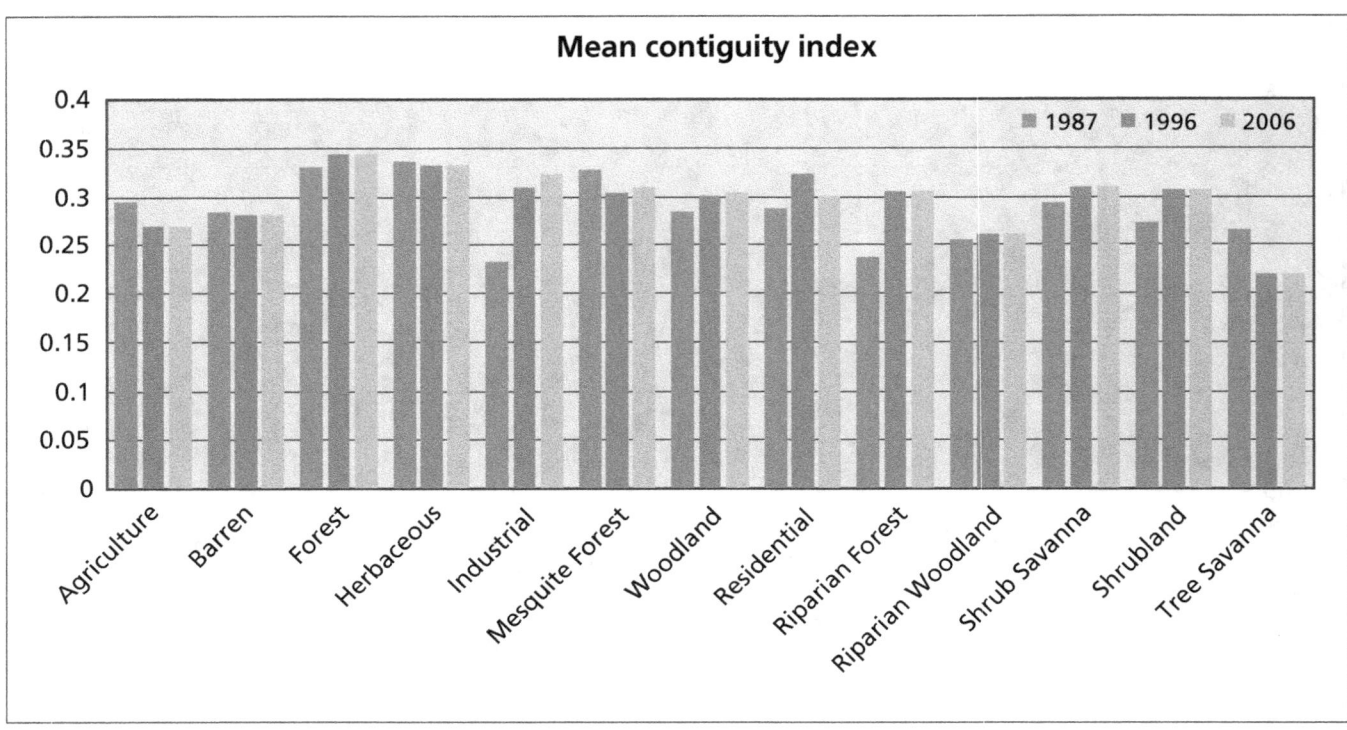

Figure 3-12. Mean contiguity index for the 1987, 1996, and 2006 land-cover maps.

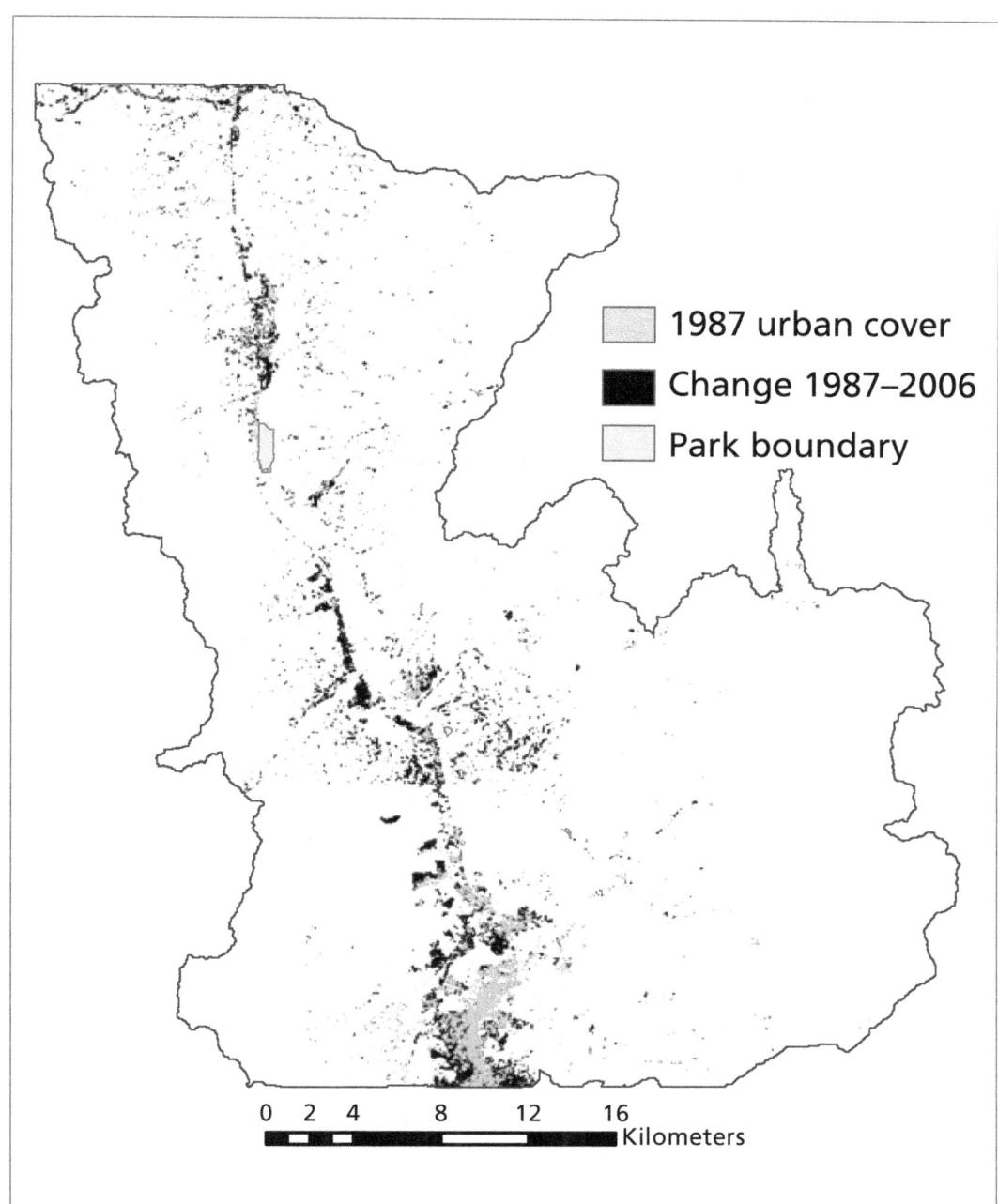

Figure 3-13. Spatial location of residential and industrial change, 1987–2006.

4 Discussion

This research examined the use of Landsat-based CART modeling and vegetation mapping from historical photography for NPS landscape dynamics monitoring. The results of this research indicate that the two approaches can provide valuable historical and spatial information for NPS monitoring programs—information that can guide management decisions and help national parks to address landscape and vegetation changes occurring within and around park boundaries.

The landscape dynamics protocol presented in this report resulted in multidecadal accuracies of over 80%, suggesting that the CART approach is reliable, repeatable, and can provide realistic data describing park landscapes. The following is a list of the advantages and outcomes of this project:

- Information on classification techniques collected thorough the remote-sensing literature review and the high accuracies of CART maps created using the methods in this report suggest that spectral transformation of multi-date imagery can help to increase class separability, resulting in high classification accuracies.

- The CART technique provides tractability of input variables via interpretation of the decision tree output.

- The high accuracies of the CART-based maps indicates that seasonal Landsat data, in combination with CART modeling, is an appropriate model for multi-decadal SODN landscape dynamics monitoring.

- Fragmentation indices and change-detection techniques allow interpretation and visualization of complex data.

Map derivatives, such as land-cover conversion and fragmentation changes between decades, are just two examples of how the methods described in this report can be used to characterize and monitor landscape dynamics.

We recommend that the following steps be taken to provide additional insights into the SODN landscape dynamics monitoring protocol and the utility of resultant products for other SODN parks and management applications:

- Analyze the CART model data to better understand the contribution of each variable and supporting biophysical mechanisms.

- Integrate land-cover maps with land-use and socio-economic datasets.

- Test the protocol on other SODN parks with different vegetation types and land-use patterns.

5 Literature Cited

Anderson, J. F., E. E. Hardy, J. T. Roach, and R. E. Witmer. 1976. A land use and land-cover classification system for use with remote sensor data. U.S. Geological Survey, Washington, D.C.

Arizona Remote Sensing Center and Sonoran Institute (ARSC&SI). 2008. Santa Cruz County riparian vegetation mapping project. Santa Cruz County, Arizona

Bernstein, R. 1983. Image geometry and rectification. Pages 873–922 in R. N. Colwell, ed., Manual of remote sensing. Second edition. American Society of Photogrammetry, Falls Church, Virginia.

Blaisdell, E. A. 1993. Statistics in practice. New York: Harcourt Brace Jovanovich.

Bruzzone, L., and S. B. Serpico. 2000. A technique for feature selection in multiclass problems. International Journal of Remote Sensing 21:549–563.

Chander, G., B. L. Markham, and J. A. Barsi. 2007. Revised Landsat-5 thematic mapper radiometric calibration. Geoscience and Remote Sensing Letters, IEEE 4:490–494.

Chavez, P. S., Jr. 1996. Image-based atmospheric corrections, revisited and improved. Photogrammetric Engineering and Remote Sensing 62:1025–1036.

Chen, L., and L. Lee. 1992. Progressive generation of control frameworks for image registration. Photogrammetric Engineering and Remote Sensing 58:1321–1328.

Cohen, W. B., and S. N. Goward. 2004. Landsat's role in ecological applications of remote sensing. Bioscience 54:535–545.

Collins, J. B., and C. E. Woodcock. 1996. An assessment of several linear change detection techniques for mapping forest mortality using multi-temporal landsat TM data. Remote Sensing of Environment 56:66–77.

Congalton, R. G., K. Birch, R. Jones, and J. Schriever. 2002. Evaluating remotely sensed techniques for mapping riparian vegetation. Computers and Electronics in Agriculture 37:113–126.

Coppin, P., I. Jonckheere, K. Nackaerts, B. Muys, and E. Lambin. 2004. Digital change detection methods in ecosystem monitoring: A review. International Journal of Remote Sensing 25:1565–1596.

Coppin, P. R., and M. E. Bauer. 1994. Processing of multi-temporal Landsat TM imagery to optimize extraction of forest cover change features. IEEE Transactions on Geoscience and Remote Sensing 32:918–927.

Crist, E. P., and R. C. Cicone. 1984. A physically-based transformation of thematic mapper data-the tm Tasseled Cap. IEEE Transactions on Geoscience and Remote Sensing 22:256–263.

Curcio, J. A. 1961. Evaluation of atmospheric aerosol particle size distribution from scattering measurement in the visible and infrared. Journal of the Optical Society of America 51:548–551.

de Colstoun, E. C. B., M. H. Story, C. Thompson, K. Commisso, T. G. Smith, and J. R. Irons. 2003. National park vegetation mapping using multi-temporal Landsat 7 data and a decision tree classifier. Remote Sensing of Environment 85:316–327.

Dikshit, O. 1996. Textural classification for ecological research using ATM images. International Journal of Remote Sensing 17:887–915.

Drake, S., S. Buckley, M.L. Villarreal, S. Studd and A.J., Hubbard. 2009. Vegetation classification, distribution and mapping report: Tumacácori National Historical Park. Natural Resource Report NPS/SODN/NRR—2009/148. National Park Service, Fort Collins, Colorado.

Federal Geographic Data Committee (FGDC). 2008. Vegetation classification standard, Version 2.0.

Florinsky, I. V. 1998. Combined analysis of digital terrain models and remotely sensed data in landscape investigations. Progress in Physical Geography 22:33–60.

Foody, G. M., N. A. Campbell, N. M. Trood, and T. F. Wood. 1992. Derivation and applications of probabilistic measures of class membership from the Maximum Likelihood Classification. Photogrammetric Engineering and Remote Sensing 58:1335–1341.

Franklin, S. E., A. J. Maudie, and M. B. Lavigne. 2001. Using spatial co-occurrence texture to increase forest structure and species composition classification accuracy. Photogrammetric Engineering and Remote Sensing 67:849–855.

Friedl, M. A., C. E. Brodley, and A. H. Strahler. 1999. Maximizing land-cover classification accuracies produced by decision trees at continental to global scales. IEEE Transactions on Geoscience and Remote Sensing 37:969–977.

Gao, B. C. 1995. Normalized difference water index for remote sensing of vegetation liquid water from space. Proceedings of the International Society for Optics and Photonics (SPIE) 2480:225–236.

Grinand, C., D. Arrouays, B. Laroche, and M. P. Martin. 2008. Extrapolating regional soil landscapes from an existing soil map: Sampling intensity, validation procedures, and integration of spatial context. Geoderma 143:180–190.

Grossman D.H., Faber-Langendoen D., Weakley A.S., Anderson M., Bourgeron P., Crawford R., Goodin K., Landaal S., Metzler K., Patterson K.D., Pyne M., Reid M., and Sneddon L. 1998. International classification of ecological communities: terrestrial vegetation of the United States. Volume I, The National Vegetation Classification System: development, status, and applications. The Nature Conservancy: Arlington, Virginia.

Gustafson, E. J., and G. R. Parker. 1992. Relationships between landcover proportion and indices of landscape spatial pattern. Landscape Ecology 7:101–110.

Hansen, M., R. Dubayah, and R. DeFries. 1996. Classification trees: An alternative to traditional land cover classifiers. International Journal of Remote Sensing 17:1075–1081.

Haralick, R. M., K. Shanmugam, and I. Dinstein. 1973. Textural features for image classification. IEEE Transactions on Systems, Man, and Cybernetics 3:610–621.

Hardisky, M. A., V. Klemas, and R. M. Smart. 1983. The influence of soil salinity, growth form, and leaf moisture on the spectral radiance of *Spartina alterniflora* canopies. Photogrammetric Engineering & Remote Sensing 49:77–83.

Huang, C., B. Wylie, L. Yang, C. Homer, and G. Zylstra. 2002. Derivation of a tasselled cap transformation based on Landsat 7 at-satellite reflectance. International Journal of Remote Sensing 23:1741–1748.

Huete, A., K. Didan, T. Miura, E. P. Rodriguez, X. Gao, and L. G. Ferreira. 2002. Overview of the radiometric and biophysical performance of the MODIS vegetation indices. Remote Sensing of Environment 83:195–213.

Huete, A. R. 1988. A soil-adjusted vegetation index (SAVI). Remote Sensing of Environment 25:295–309.

Hutchinson, C. F. 1982. Techniques for combining Landsat and ancillary data for digital classification improvement. Photogrammetric Engineering and Remote Sensing 48:123–130.

Jensen, J. R. 1996. Introductory digital image processing. Second edition. Upper Saddle River, N.J.: Prentice Hall.

Jiang, Z., A. R. Huete, K. Didan, and T. Miura. 2008. Development of a two-band enhanced vegetation index without a blue band. Remote Sensing of Environment 112:3833–3845.

Kauth, R. J., P. F. Lambeck, W. Richardson, G. S. Thomas, and A. P. Pentland. 1979. Feature extraction applied to agricultural crops as seen by Landsat. Pages 705–721 *in* The LACIE symposium: Proceedings of technical sessions. NASA Johnson Space Center, Houston, Texas.

Kauth, R. J., and G. S. Thomas. 1976. The tasseled cap: A graphic description of the spectral-temporal development of agricultural crops as seen in Landsat. Pages 41–51 *in* Proceedings of the symposium on machine processing of remotely sensed data, West Lafayette, Indiana, June 29–July 1, 1976. Laboratory for Applications of Remote Sensing, Purdue University, West Lafayette, Indiana.

Kuo, B. C., and D. A. Landgrebe. 2004. Nonparametric weighted feature extraction for classification. IEEE Transactions on Geoscience and Remote Sensing 42:1096–1105.

LaGro, J., Jr. 1991. Assessing patch shape in landscape mosaics. Photogrammetric Engineering & Remote Sensing 57:285–293.

Lawrence, R., A. Bunn, S. Powell, and M. Zambon. 2004. Classification of remotely sensed imagery using stochastic gradient boosting as a refinement of classification tree analysis. Remote Sensing of Environment 90:331–336.

Lawrence, R. L., and A. Wright. 2001. Rule-based classification systems using classification and regression tree (CART) analysis. Photogrammetric Engineering & Remote Sensing 67:1137–1142.

Lowry, J., R. D. Ramsey, K. Thomas, D. Schrupp, T. Sajwaj, J. Kirby, E. Waller, S. Schrader, S. Falzarano, L. Langs, G. Manis, C. Wallace, K. Schulz, P. Comer, K. Pohs, W. Rieth, C. Velasquez, B. Wolk, W. Kepner, K. Boykin, L. O'Brien, D. Bradford, B. Thompson, and J. Prior-Magee. 2007. Mapping moderate-scale land-cover over very large geographic areas within a collaborative framework: A case study of the Southwest Regional Gap Analysis Project (SWReGAP). Remote Sensing of Environment 108:59–73.

Lu, D., P. Mausel, E. Brondizio, and E. Moran. 2004. Change detection techniques. International Journal of Remote Sensing 25:2365–2407.

Lu, D., and Q. Weng. 2007. A survey of image classification methods and techniques for improving classification performance. International Journal of Remote Sensing 28:823–870.

Marsett, R. C., J. Qi, P. Heilman, S. H. Biedenbender, M. C. Watson, S. Amer, M. Weltz, D. Goodrich, and R. MarsettI. 2006. Remote Sensing for Grassland Management in the Arid Southwest. Rangeland Ecology & Management 59:530–540.

Maynard, C. L., R. L. Lawrence, G. A. Nielsen, and G. Decker. 2007. Ecological site descriptions and remotely sensed imagery as a tool for rangeland evaluation. Canadian Journal of Remote Sensing 33:109–115.

McBratney, A. B., M. L. Mendonca Santos, and B. Minasny. 2003. On digital soil mapping. Geoderma 117:3–52.

McGarigal, K., S. A. Cushman, M. C. Neel, and E. Ene. 2002. FRAGSTATS: Spatial pattern analysis program for categorical maps. http://www.umass.edu/landeco/research/fragstats/fragstats.html.

Munoz-Villers, L. E., and J. Lopez-Blanco. 2008. Land use/cover changes using Landsat TM/ETM images in a tropical and biodiverse mountainous area of central-eastern Mexico. International Journal of Remote Sensing 29:71–93.

Pal, M., and P. M. Mather. 2003. An assessment of the effectiveness of decision tree methods for land cover classification. Remote Sensing of Environment 86:554–565.

Peddle, D. R., and S. E. Franklin. 1991. Image texture processing and data integration for surface pattern-discrimination. Photogrammetric Engineering and Remote Sensing 57:413–420.

Prasad, A., L. Iverson, and A. Liaw. 2006. Newer classification and regression tree techniques: Bagging and random forests for ecological prediction. Ecosystems 9:181–199.

Qi, J., A. Chehbouni, A. R. Huete, Y. H. Kerr, and S. Sorooshian. 1994. A modified soil adjusted vegetation index. Remote Sensing of Environment 48:119–126.

Quinlan, J. R. 1996. Bagging, boosting and C4.5. Pages 725–730 in Proceedings of the 13th national conference on artificial intelligence. Portland, Ore.: AAAI Press.

Roberts, D. A., I. Numata, K. Holmes, G. Batista, T. Krug, A. Monteiro, B. Powell, and O. A. Chadwick. 2002. Large area mapping of land-cover change in Rondonia using multitemporal spectral mixture analysis and decision tree classifiers. Journal of Geophysical Research-Atmospheres 107 (40-1–40-18).

Rogan, J., and S. R. Yool. 2001. Mapping fire-induced vegetation depletion in the Peloncillo Mountains, Arizona and New Mexico. International Journal of Remote Sensing 22:3101–3121.

Shalaby, A., and R. Tateishi. 2007. Remote sensing and GIS for mapping and monitoring land cover and land-use changes in the Northwestern coastal zone of Egypt. Applied Geography 27:28–41.

Sibins, F. F. 1978. Remote sensing principles and interpretation, San Francisco, Ca.: Freeman.

Slater, P. N., F. J. Doyle, N. L. Fritz, and R. Welch., eds. 1983. Photographic systems for remote sensing: Manual of remote sensing. Second edition. American Society of Photogrammetrty, Falls Church, Virginia.

Sohn, Y., and J. G. Qi. 2005. Mapping detailed biotic communities in the upper San Pedro Valley of Southeastern Arizona using Landsat 7 ETM+ data and supervised spectral angle classifier. Photogrammetric Engineering and Remote Sensing 71:709–718.

Steyaert, L. T., and R. G. Knox. 2008. Reconstructed historical land cover and biophysical parameters for studies of land-atmosphere interactions within the eastern United States. Journal of Geophysical Research-Atmospheres 113, D02101, 27 pp.

Swain, P. H., and S. M. Davis. 1978. Remote sensing: The quantitative approach. New York: McGraw-Hill.

Thenkabail, P. S., E. A. Enclona, M. S. Ashton, C. Legg, and M. J. De Dieu. 2004. Hyperion, IKONOS, ALI, and ETM plus sensors in the study of African rainforests. Remote Sensing of Environment 90:23–43.

Turner, R. E., W. A. Malila , and R. F. Nalepha. 1971. Importance of atmospheric scattering in remote sensing. Pages 1651–1697 *in* Proceedings of the 7th International Symposium on Remote Sensing of the Environment, Ann Arbor, Michigan.

Vogelmann, J. E., T. L. Sohl, P. V. Campbell, and D. M. Shaw. 1998. Regional land cover characterization using Landsat thematic mapper data and ancillary data sources. Environmental Monitoring and Assessment 51:415–428.

Whitcomb, R., C. Robbins, J. Lynch, B. Whitcomb, M. Klimkiewicz, and D. Bystrak. 1981. Effects of forest fragmentation on avifauna of the eastern deciduous forest. Ecological Studies. Vol. 41, 1981, pp. 125 – 206 Wilson, E. H., and S. A. Sader. 2002. Detection of forest harvest type using multiple dates of Landsat TM imagery. Remote Sensing of Environment 80:385–396.

Yang, X. 2007. Integrated use of remote sensing and geographic information systems in riparian vegetation delineation and mapping. International Journal of Remote Sensing 28:353–370.

Yang, X., and C. P. Lo. 2002. Using a time series of satellite imagery to detect land use and land cover changes in the Atlanta, Georgia metropolitan area. International Journal of Remote Sensing 23:1775–1798.

Yang, X. J., and C. P. Lo. 2000. Relative radiometric normalization performance for change detection from multi-date satellite images. Photogrammetric Engineering and Remote Sensing 66:967–980.

Zhou, Q., B. Li, and A. Kurban. 2008. Trajectory analysis of land cover change in arid environment of China. International Journal of Remote Sensing 29:1093–1107.

Appendix A. Results and Accuracy Assessments

Results, accuracy assessments, and Kappa statistics (representing the accuracy of the classes based on the training data used to generate the classification from the data-layer stacks). Errors are shown in red.

Table A1. Accuracy matrices for supervised tests (Year 2006).

Class #	Class name	1	2	3	4	5	6	7	8	9	10	11	12	13	14	Total	User's accuracy
Test 1																	
1	Agriculture	20	6		8	1	19	5	1	13	8		1	4	18	104	0.19
2	Barren		0													0	
3	Forest			0												0	
4	Herbaceous				0											0	
5	Industrial					0										0	
6	Mesquite forest						0									0	
7	Mesquite woodland		6	25	5	2	7	37	5	15	20	18	24	18	18	200	0.19
8	Residential		15		1	29			16			1	3		2	67	0.24
9	Riparian forest									0						0	
10	Riparian woodland										0					0	
11	Shrub savanna											0				0	
12	Shrubland		4		7			1	2			7	13	1		35	0.37
13	Tree savanna													0		0	
14	Water														0	0	
	Total	20	31	25	21	32	26	43	24	28	28	26	41	23	38	406	
	Producer's accuracy	1.00	0.00	0.00	0.00	0.00	0.00	0.86	0.67	0.00	0.00	0.00	0.32	0.00	0.00		
	Overall accuracy	21.18															
	Kappa	0.1402															

Table A1. Accuracy matrices for supervised tests (Year 2006), cont.

Class #	Class name	1	2	3	4	5	6	7	8	9	10	11	12	13	14	Total	User's accuracy
Test 2																	
1	Agriculture	15			4		16	4		3	11	1		5	1	60	0.25
2	Barren		0													0	
3	Forest			0												0	
4	Herbaceous	3	1		12		1			1		6	3			27	0.44
5	Industrial					0										0	
6	Mesquite forest						0									0	
7	Mesquite woodland		3	25	2		3	32		13	17	7	20	17		139	0.23
8	Residential	2	24		5	32	1	2	22	4		9	3		33	137	0.16
9	Riparian forest						6			8						14	0.57
10	Riparian woodland										0					0	
11	Shrub savanna											0				0	
12	Shrubland	1	4		8			4	2			11	18	1		49	0.37
13	Tree savanna													0		0	
14	Water														0	0	
	Total	21	32	25	31	32	26	43	24	28	29	34	44	23	34	426	
	Producer's accuracy	*0.71*	*0.00*	*0.00*	*0.39*	*0.00*	*0.00*	*0.74*	*0.92*	*0.29*	*0.00*	*0.00*	*0.41*	*0.00*	*0.00*		
	Overall accuracy	*25.12*															
	Kappa	*0.189*															

Table A1. Accuracy matrices for supervised tests (Year 2006), cont.

Class #	Class name	1	2	3	4	5	6	7	8	9	10	11	12	13	14	Total	User's accuracy
Test 3																	
1	Agriculture	14			1			1	1		3			3	15	39	0.36
2	Barren		0													0	
3	Forest			17				2								19	0.89
4	Herbaceous	3	1		9			1			2					16	0.56
5	Industrial		1		1	20				1						23	0.87
6	Mesquite forest						16			1	1					18	0.89
7	Mesquite woodland	1		8	4	2	2	30	2	2	5	5	16	12	18	107	0.28
8	Residential		18		2	10	2	2	19	5	2	3	2			68	0.28
9	Riparian forest	1					3	2		19	1					26	0.73
10	Riparian woodland						2	1			11		1			14	0.79
11	Shrub savanna		3		3							13	2	1		23	0.57
12	Shrubland		8		5			2				2	17	1		39	0.44
13	Tree savanna		1		6			2			2	11	6	6		34	0.18
14	Water														0	0	
	Total	21	32	25	31	32	26	43	24	28	29	34	44	23	34	426	
	Producer's accuracy	0.67	0.00	0.68	0.29	0.63	0.62	0.70	0.79	0.68	0.38	0.38	0.39	0.26	0.00		
	Overall accuracy	44.84															
	Kappa	0.4035															

Class	Class name	1	2	3	4	5	6	7	8	9	10	11	12	13	14	Total	User's accuracy
2006																	
1	Agriculture	20			3		1	1						2		27	0.74
2	Barren		13						2							15	0.87
3	Forest			23				1								24	0.96
4	Herbaceous	2			22			1				3	1	1		30	0.73
5	Industrial		1			27			1							29	0.93
6	Mesquite Forest						29								1	30	0.97
7	Woodland			1				20	1		2	1	3	1		29	0.69
8	Residential		4		1	4			19						1	29	0.66
9	Riparian Forest									25	2					27	0.93
10	Riparian Woodland						2				26		1			29	0.90
11	Shrub Savanna				1							25	2	2		30	0.83
12	Shrubland		3					1				2	23	1		30	0.77
13	Tree Savanna				1			1					4	24		30	0.80
14	Water														30	30	1.00
	Total	22	21	24	28	31	32	25	23	25	30	31	34	31	32	389	
	Producer's accuracy	0.91	0.62	0.96	0.79	0.87	0.91	0.80	0.83	1.00	0.87	0.81	0.68	0.77	0.94		
	Overall accuracy	83.8															
	Kappa	0.83															

Table A2. CART accuracy matrices, cont.

Class	Class name	1	2	3	4	5	6	7	8	9	10	11	12	13	14	Total	User's accuracy
1996																	
1	Agriculture	24						2		1		1	2			30	0.80
2	Barren		26						2			1	1			30	0.87
3	Forest			29				1								30	0.97
4	Herbaceous	1	2		18			1				3	3	2		30	0.60
5	Industrial		1			26			1				2			30	0.87
6	Mesquite Forest						27	2		1						30	0.90
7	Woodland			3				26						1		30	0.87
8	Residential		2					3	20				3	2		30	0.67
9	Riparian Forest			2			2	3		23						30	0.77
10	Riparian Woodland		1				3	2			23			1		30	0.77
11	Shrub Savanna											26		3	1	30	0.87
12	Shrubland							1	1			3	25			30	0.83
13	Tree Savanna							1				2		27		30	0.90
14	Water												1	2	27	30	0.90
	Total	25	32	34	18	26	32	42	24	25	23	36	37	38	28	420	
	Producer's accuracy	0.96	0.81	0.85	1.00	1.00	0.84	0.62	0.83	0.92	1.00	0.72	0.68	0.71	0.96		
	Overall accuracy	82.6															
	Kappa	0.81															

Table A2. CART accuracy matrices, cont.

1987

Class	Class name	1	2	3	4	5	6	7	8	9	10	11	12	13	14	Total	User's accuracy
1	Agriculture	33			1			1								35	0.94
2	Barren		32													32	1.00
3	Forest			18				1								19	0.95
4	Herbaceous				52			4						6		62	0.84
5	Industrial					30			1						1	32	0.94
6	Mesquite Forest						35			1						36	0.97
7	Woodland			1	2			34			1		1	3		41	0.83
8	Residential		10		3			1	27		1		1	1	1	45	0.60
9	Riparian Forest						3	3	1	28			1			34	0.82
10	Riparian Woodland				1		3				26		1			35	0.74
11	Shrub Savanna				2							27				31	0.87
12	Shrubland				1			3				4	58	2	1	69	0.84
13	Tree Savanna				4							1		16		21	0.76
14	Water														28	28	1.00
	Total	35	42	19	66	31	41	47	29	29	28	32	62	28	31	520	
	Producer's accuracy	0.94	0.76	0.95	0.79	0.97	0.85	0.72	0.93	0.97	0.93	0.84	0.94	0.57	0.90		
	Overall accuracy	85.38															
	Kappa	0.84															

NPS 960/110599, September 2011

National Park Service
U.S. Department of the Interior

Natural Resource Stewardship and Science
1201 Oak Ridge Drive, Suite 150
Fort Collins, Colorado 80525

www.nature.nps.gov

EXPERIENCE YOUR AMERICA™